Walks Around the Malverns

Roy Woodcock

Meridian Books

Published 1997 by Meridian Books
Second edition 2005

© Roy Woodcock 1997, 2005

ISBN 1-869922-53-0

A catalogue record for this book is available from the British Library.

Meridian Books
40 Hadzor Road, Oldbury, West Midlands B68 9LA

Printed in Great Britain by Cromwell Press, Trowbridge, Wiltshire

Contents

Three walks from Wynds Point

Two walks from Hollybush

Three walks from Ledbury

Four Walks from Upton upon Severn

Introduction

BEING fortunate enough to live in Great Malvern at the foot of the hills it is always tempting to have a walk on this famous range of very old rocks. Also, as there appeared to be no book of Malvern Hills walks available in the shops it seemed sensible to try and rectify this deficiency.

There are several books of walks which contain one or two in the Malvern area, and there are pamphlets of individual walks, but I thought that the hills and commons around Malvern were worth much more than that. There are well over a hundred miles of paths on the hills and commons, and there is almost unlimited walking with real *freedom to roam* over many hectares of countryside. Much of this is thanks to the work of the Malvern Hills Conservators who have looked after this piece of countryside for more than a hundred years.

The hills are prominent from far afield, for example while driving on the M5 or standing on the edge of the Cotswolds scarp looking westwards or from hills in the Welsh borders looking eastwards. The hills are magnificent and the ridge walk is one of the finest in the country, with views east and west over large areas of rural England and into Wales.

The walks were selected to cover the entire range of hills and the adjacent commons; and, as the views looking at the hills can be as impressive as those looking from the hills, a few walks in the Ledbury area to the west and the Upton area to the east were added. This completed the all round views to and from this steep and narrow ridge of hills which stand up so dramatically from the Severn plain.

All along the ridge there are steep slopes to climb if desired and these provide energetic walking with new views every few minutes – and near aerial views looking down across the plain. But in addition to the steep paths there are many fairly gentle walks and several miles of surfaced paths which could be used by wheelchairs. Some of the car parks created by the Conservators are quite high up on the hillside, for example at West Malvern Quarries, near the Wyche Cutting and at Earnslaw Quarry.

Most of the paths remain fairly firm and dry even in wet weather, but can be slippery or stony in places. Sensible footwear is essential, especially in winter when conditions can become quite icy. Winds are often very strong and warm clothing is essential. Do not be fooled by the milder weather conditions down on the plain or in the town. The woods on the lower slopes of the hills can be relied on to give shelter if required, but the exposed bare hill top often has the weather of a more mountainous environment than its height would suggest.

My thanks go to Peter Groves and Des Wright for careful checking of the walks to ensure accuracy of detail. Thanks also to Margaret for accompanying me on most of the walks, as well as checking details and most careful proof reading. Also thanks to Wendy for the drawings which improve the general layout and appearance of the book as well as showing a few of the many interesting features shown on the walks. The photograph on page 81 is by Peter Groves and is reproduced with permission from his book *Heritage Discovery Walks in the Midlands*.

I hope you will enjoy this book and be rewarded with wonderful fresh air and some of the stunning views for which the Malverns are noted.

Roy Woodcock
Great Malvern

Using this book

THE walks in this book range from 2½ to 10 miles, with a longer option of 16 miles for walk 5. Some are on level ground, some feature fairly modest ascents and others (inevitably, given the nature of the Malvern Hills) involve fairly steep climbs and undulating terrain.

The sketch maps accompanying each walk are intended to serve as guidance and not as replacements for the appropriate Ordnance Survey maps. Even though you may not always need to use them they are invaluable if in emergency, bad weather or other reason you wish to cut short or re-route your walk. The best map to have is the Ordnance Survey Explorer map 190 which at a scale of 1:25,00 (2½ miles to the inch) covers the whole of the area included in this book. In the introduction box at the start of each walk you will find grid references for the starting points, car parking details and other useful information.

It is always sensible to carry a compass, to have good footwear, preferably good quality walking boots, and adequate waterproofs. A basic first aid kit should also be carried. Although the introduction box lists sources of refreshment it is advisable to carry some food and drink – this can give you some extra independence.

With one exception all the walks are circular and for walks 11, 12, 13 and possibly 5, a car is necessary to reach the starting point. However, all the others can be followed by using train and/or bus and in these cases details are given in the information box. Details of routes and times (which should always be checked before you set out) can be obtained from:

Rail enquiries: www.nationalrail.co.uk
08457 484950

All forms of public transport www.traveline.org.uk
0870 6082608

All forms of travel, both public transport and road
www.transportdirect.info
At the time of writing this was still in development.

The Geology of the Malverns

THE rocks of the Malverns are hard, which is why the landscape is so steep. There are igneous rocks which have been formed by volcanic activity, and there are some metamorphic rocks too. These were either sedimentary or igneous rocks which have been changed as a result of heat or pressure affecting them. All the Malvern rocks are so old that they formed before life existed on earth, so there are no fossils in the main ridge of hills. This is not true of lands just to the west, in Herefordshire, where ridges of Silurian limestones are richly fossiliferous in places.

Several east-west faults cut through the ridge, and they can best be seen in the gaps running across the hills. These gaps are followed by the routeways such as the Wyche, Wynds or Gullet. Younger Silurian rocks which lie alongside the Malvern ridge were crumpled up by the earth movements of Caledonian time, which also caused many faults. The Herefordshire Beacon was moved to the west of the main ridge at this time. Later earth movements, called the Hercynian, created the main trend of the Malvern ridge as well as other north-south ridges in the U.K.

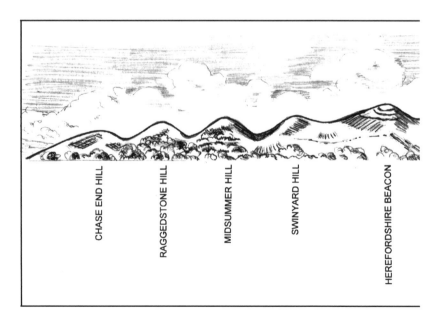

Some of the metamorphic rocks date from before 1200 million years ago, and there was considerable volcanic activity which formed some of the rocks between 1200 and 600 million years ago.

The main rocks are called Malvernian type and contain many types of igneous and metamorphic rocks, and no two rocks are identical. There are many variations of metamorphic rocks, mainly schists and gneisses, which make up about 5% of the total area. Igneous rocks were intruded into these older metamorphic rocks, and they represent about 75% of the Malvernian complex of rocks. These include several types of granite and also diorites. The remaining 20% is younger igneous rocks, notably dolerites.

A few examples of the variations in the Malvernian rocks are:

North Hill and the Worcestershire Beacon contain igneous rocks such as diorite and hornblende granite.

The Herefordshire Beacon is mostly gneiss with some basalt on the north side. Swinyard Hill is gneiss with diorite and some hornblende granite.

Midsummer and Hollybush Hills are gneiss and schist.

Raggedstone Hill is schist although there is some quartzite too.

Chase End Hill is hornblende gneiss.

Pegmatite veins are common, for example in Gullet Quarry.

Dolerite and other basic intrusions occur for example in Dingle Quarry, Tank Quarry, North Hill and Gullet Quarry.

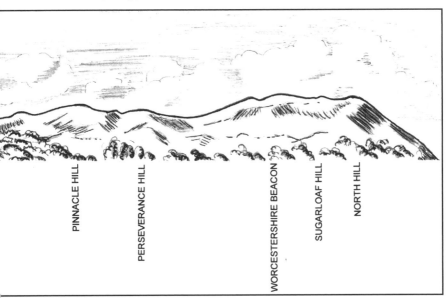

A profile of the Malverns

Whereas the Malvernian rocks occupy most of the hill range, there is an area of the Warren House Volcanic group of rocks to the east of the Herefordshire Beacon on Hangman's Hill, Broad Down and Tinker's Hill, and they include basalts, some rhyolite, tuff and dolerite. These rocks dip down to the east and rest unconformably on the Malvernian rocks. Therefore they are younger than the Malvernian but are still pre-Cambrian in age. They are probably Uriconian which means they are similar in age to some rocks in Shropshire. The eastern edge of these Uriconian rocks is a fault line, beyond which is the Triassic area of the Severn Plain. There is also a major fault along the western side of the Malvern rocks near the Herefordshire border.

There are some younger Cambrian rocks in the Malvern area. These include Lower Cambrian quartzites at the northern end of Midsummer Hill. There are also conglomerates, rhyolites and andesites with these quartzites.

The Lower Cambrian Hollybush sandstone is on top of the Malvern quartzites (and therefore younger) and contains sandstone which is often flaggy and glauconitic, with some thin calcareous layers. The Upper Cambrian Whiteleaved Oak shales contain black shales and some grit. These are younger than the other rocks mentioned and do contain some fossils.

There were many igneous intrusions in the southern Malverns during the Cambrian period about 550 million years ago, e.g. basalts and andesites.

The Malverns were an island ridge 400-500 million years ago, surrounded by a tropical sea. Silurian rocks were being deposited along the shore, and a large area of these is exposed to the west of the main ridge. There is a succession of shallow and deeper water sediments, mainly sandstones, shales and limestones. Sandstones and limestones generally form ridges and the shales form valleys, creating the undulating landscape. These rocks have been crumpled by folding and are often nearly vertical, therefore having only narrow outcrops. As they contain fossils, much more is known about them than the Malvernian.

At a later time, other younger rocks may have covered the surrounding land and possibly covered the whole Malvern ridge as well. There has been erosion for millions of years to wear away all the softer surrounding rocks and leave the Malverns upstanding.

There is still surprisingly little known about the Malvern rocks themselves. There are several quarries where rocks can be seen, but what is there underneath? The Colwall railway tunnel exposed some rocks, as did a well at the Malvern Hills Hotel at Wynds, but there is still much to be learned about the origin of the rocks.

Weather on the Malverns

TWO aspects of weather worthy of particular mention are the wind and the visibility. Sun and rain are other important meteorological phenomena but are more obvious and perhaps less in need of a mention. Sun is slightly less than on the surrounding lowlands simply because the hills are cloudier and wetter. It is possible to have drizzle on the hills when it is fine below, or to have heavier rain on the hills when it is only drizzling down on the plain.

The hills are likely to be very windy and, except in mid summer, may feel unpleasantly cold – so warm clothing is essential. In spite of the lack of elevation there is often a big temperature difference between the foot of the hills and the exposed top of the ridge. Windward and leeward locations will vary depending on wind direction. Both sides may be equally windy with northerly or southerly winds,, but otherwise one side of the ridge is likely to be sheltered and the other side very exposed. Rounding corners or going over the top of the ridge will reveal startling differences and may be quite breath taking, and capable of blowing small children over.

Visibility may be very restricted, and in wet weather, once on the top, visibility may be virtually nil. With cloud spread all around, it is like being on an island suspended in space. On sunny days, the haze will often restrict visibility to only a mile or so. Views tend to be better in the mornings than in the afternoons. However some good views to the west may occur in the evenings as the sun sinks down behind the Welsh hills. The best visibility tends to come on the windy and showery days. After a clearing shower of rain it is possible to see as much as 40-50 miles. North westerly airstreams are particularly good for giving these clear viewing days.

The Malvern Hills Conservators

THE Board of Conservators contains both elected and nominated members, including members of the local District and County Councils. The Malvern Hills Conservators look after approximately 3000 acres for the benefit of visitors and local residents. They maintain land both on the hills and on adjacent commons. Sources of money are the County Council, the Countryside Commisssion and car parking fees – the last source is growing steadily and adding a useful sum to the income. Local residents pay a precept on the Council Tax, which is the main source of income.

M.H.C. is an independent body which was originally formed by Act of Parliament in 1884. It was one of Britain's earliest groups of conservationists. Hillside quarries were bought and work was halted just in time to prevent the skyline profile of the Malverns from being changed. Several of the quarries have been shielded by tree planting efforts, and are being used as car parks and picnic areas. In the last twenty years rehabilitation work has been in progress in Tank Quarry (managed by the County Council) in the north and Gullet Quarry in the south.

Evidence of the M.H.C. work can be seen in many other places too. Footpath mowing, footpath restoration, parking facilities, scrub clearance, woodland control, tree planting, provision of seats, notices and information, are all part of this work. As there are more than a million visitors to the hills in a year, the whole area would be destroyed and devastated without the efforts of the M.H.C.

By law it is the duty of the Conservators to prevent encroachment on to their lands and to keep them open for recreation and enjoyment.

A recent major development in July 1995, was the new Act which gives the Conservators extra powers. The Malvern Hills Bill became law after five years of negotiations. The Conservators can now license up to six refreshment stalls if they wish, but will not be allowed to rebuild the cafe at the Worcestershire Beacon. They can also close off parts of the hills if necessary, and can restrict horse riding. Sheep and cattle have recently been reintroduced to the hills to help preserve open views and grassland habitat.

In order to make decisions and consider future plans, the Conservators meet bi-monthly, and all meetings are open to the public, unless sensitive legal or financial matters are under discussion. The Conservators have a website: www.malvernhills.org.uk.

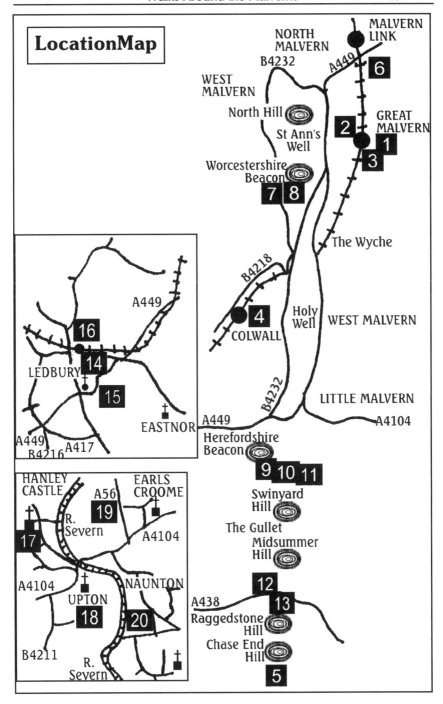

Five Malvern Walks

GREAT MALVERN developed around the eleventh century Priory of Malvern Magna, but remained fairly small until the time of the Water Cure which gave a great boost to the town's growth. Hydrotherapy was developed by Doctor Wilson and Doctor Gully, using an idea brought in from Austria, and during Victorian times Great Malvern grew rapidly as a Spa town. The spring water had already been made famous in the eighteenth century, notably by Doctor John Wall. In 1757 he analysed the spring water and found it to be very pure.

> The Malvern water says Dr. John Wall,
> Is famed for containing just nothing at all.

Subsequent growth of the town was associated with a large number of schools as it became an important educational town, and from the 1940s onwards a major employer was the Radar Research Unit, formerly called the D.R.A., the Defence Research Agency, and now renamed Qinetic.

Great Malvern is one of seven settlements which make up Malvern, the other six being Malvern Link, West Malvern, North Malvern, Malvern Wells, Little Malvern and The Wyche. They are all dominated by the line of hills, one of the outstanding ridges of Central England, and an important component of the town motto. '*Levavi meos oculos in montes* – I will lift up mine eyes unto the hills'. The name of Malvern is also related to the hills, being derived from moel bryn or moel vern, meaning the bare hill.

Great Malvern is easily reached by bus or train, and the A449 and A4104 give good road links to Worcester, Hereford and the M5 and M50.

Statue of Sir Edward Elgar in the Malvern Theatre

Malvern Theatres

1

Malvern Town Walk

A Victorian Journey

The station, a letter box, gas lamps, the buildings of St. Ann's Well and the fine buildings on Belle Vue Terrace are impressive reminders of Victorian times – a golden period in the development of Malvern. The walk is on roads and good paths, with one steep climb.

Distance: 3 miles (5km).
Maps: Landranger 150; Explorer 190.
Car Parking: Several car parks in Great Malvern.
Public Transport: Buses and trains to Great Malvern.
Start/Finish: Great Malvern railway station (GR783457).
Refreshments: Several possible sources of refreshment in the town.

THE STATION is worthy of close inspection before setting off on the walk. Note particularly the cast iron columns supporting the roof, with each column having an individual design in painted metal. There is a Victorian post box on the station as well as an old gas lamp, and the Lady Foley Tearooms too. At the main road is the imposing Imperial Hotel, formerly the station hotel with its own entrance to the station, but now the main building of Malvern Girls College.

Turn left along Avenue Road and walk up into the town centre. Avenue Road leads straight on to Church Street, the main shopping street, and near the top of this fairly steep climb, on the left, is the Malvern Priory church, founded in 1085 as a Benedictine Priory. Several Norman fragments still survive, and there is much which dates from the reconstruction of the fifteenth century. It escaped destruction at the time of Henry VIII in the sixteenth century, when the local people purchased the church from the Crown, and most of the church dates from that time. There are Norman pillars and arches, old tiles, and magnificent windows, with more fifteenth century stained glass than any church in England except for York Minster. In the choir area are two rows of Monks' Stalls, with some fine misericords.

From the Priory continue up Church Street and turn left by the modern Post Office to reach the Abbey Gate House Museum, housed in a fifteenth century building. The gateway is the only remnant of the monastery. The museum shows much of the local history and geology, and is open every day, for a modest entrance fee, from Easter to October (except Wednesdays during term time).

Return to Church Street and walk on up to Belle Vue Terrace where several old buildings have survived from Victorian times. At the right hand end is Barclays Bank, formerly the Library, and nearly opposite this is W.H.Smith, occupying the former Post Office and stopping place for the stage coach on the Worcester to Ledbury Highway. To the right of Smiths is the Robson Ward furniture shop, and in the courtyard

The Elgar statue in the Belle Vue Gardens

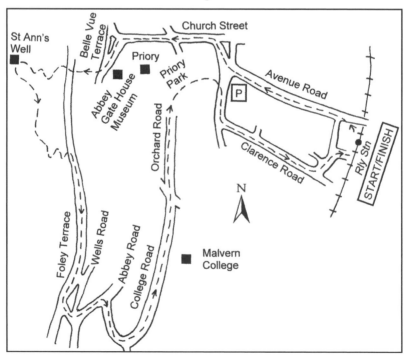

The Malvhina Spring in the Belle Vue Gardens

here is one of Malvern's many springs. Notice the recent additions of Malvhina Spring and the Elgar Statue in the Belle Vue Gardens.

Turn left and walk along Belle Vue Terrace to the Mount Pleasant Hotel, one of the hotels used in the nineteenth century Water Cure.

The Water Cure, or hydrotherapy, began in 1842 and it turned Malvern from a small village into a Spa town. Dr.Wilson set up his practice on Belle Vue Terrace, where Lloyds Bank is now situated, and Dr. Gully was along the road towards Malvern Wells, in the Tudor House next door to Warwick House. The patients were wrapped in wet sheets at 6 a.m. for about an hour, before being sent on a walk up to St. Ann's Well to drink the water before breakfast. They paid money for this, and it was claimed to do them good!

Walk alongside the Mount Pleasant Hotel on the pathway signposted to St. Ann's Well and the Worcestershire Way. At the first step is an old gas lamp, one of nearly 100 remaining in use. Looking back downhill from here there is already a view across the plain and this changes and improves with increasing height. Climb the 95 steps (traditionally known as the 99 steps!). At the top keep going on a driveway, but after 30 yards take the second turn left, along the surfaced track with an iron railing to the left and a granite wall to the right. Follow this as it zigzags up quite steeply to St. Ann's Well.

Cottagers had lived at the site of the well since the thirteenth century, but it was in the eighteenth century when visitors began to come for the water. The main buildings were constructed from 1815-1819, and popularity gradually increased. During the 1850s, the busiest period, a German band often played here in the summer months. More famous was the local man George Pullen, known as Blind George, who played the harmonium here for about 50 years.

Inside the well is a plaque with a verse written by W. Blake Atkinson, who was the Rector of Bradley near Redditch.

> Drink of this Crystal Fountain
> And Praise the Loving Lord
> Who From the Rocky Mountain
> This Living Stream Out Poured
> Fit Emblem of the Holy Fount
> That Flows from God's Eternal Mount.

St Ann's Well

Turn left at the side of St. Ann's Well, passing the toilet block and take the horizontal track. Note the excellent views to the left over Malvern and across to the Cotswolds. There are some huge trees which clothe the steep slope, and block much of the view in summer. When a path down to the left is reached, follow this downhill.

After about 50 yards bend sharply left, and then soon bend right where it is joined by a path coming in from the left, and follow the zigzag path downhill. At a minor road, turn right along Foley Terrace, to where it joins the Great Malvern – Wyche Cutting main road. Cross over on to a short stretch of minor road, which goes down to the next road. Go straight across this and turn left along Abbey Road. Pass Hillstone and Ellerslie House on the left, part of Malvern College, and then Margaret Prior House on the right and Hillstone Pre Prep on the corner where we turn right along College Road.

Follow the road round as it bends left, passing the Headmaster's House, a fine old granite structure, to then go alongside the magnificent stone buildings of Malvern College to the right of the road. The College was opened in 1865, but was evacuated for a time during World War II, when the Radar Research Establishment moved in here for vital research which led to the improvements in Radar and the British defence systems. C. S. Lewis is an old boy of the College, and although Malvern may not have been his Narnia or inspired him to think of a Wardrobe, it could certainly have given him ideas for the Lamp Post.

Walk along the length of College Road and pass the former Catholic Church of St. Joseph, Our Lady and St. Edmunds which has recently been bought by Malvern College, then go straight across on to Orchard Road. Pass the unusual Victorian pillar box, dating from 1857, and continue into Priory Park, which was formerly Dr. Gully's garden. The park contains many unusual trees, Cedar of Lebanon, wellingtonia, ginko, tulip tree, magnolia, Judas tree, mulberry, and a pocket handkerchief or dove tree.

Turn right in the park, immediately passing a small rockery/water garden, fed by a chalybeate spring, and then go left along the main drive. On the big lawn to the left were until recently busts of Sir Edward Elgar (1857-1934) and Jenny Lind (1820-1887). Sir Edward Elgar's bust was sculpted by Hilary Carruthers and bought by public subscription in 1958 to mark the centenary of his birth. Both busts are now on show inside the theatre.

The main buildings of what was formerly known as the Winter Gardens are to the left and the bandstand to the right. The Malvern Festival was centred in the Winter Gardens, in the theatre made famous by Elgar and George Bernard

Victorian bandstand in Priory Park

Shaw. The Festival was created by Sir Barry Jackson and was first held in 1929. In the early years it was very much a Shaw Festival, and J. B. Priestley was also a regular visitor to see his plays produced. There was a break during World War II, after which there were several years of an Elgar Festival. The modern Festival has been held annually since 1977, and its fame as a cultural centre enables it to draw a wide range of plays and music. There is no longer a specific festival as the theatre was completely rebuilt in 1997-98 using a grant from the National Lottery. The renamed Malvern Theatres now have a much larger and top quality programme, drawing visitors from a wide area.

Pass near the bandstand and over the footbridge across Swan Pool, formerly the Monks' fish pond. Turn left, then swing right round the Leisure Complex and, passing the fine Malvern Hills Council House on the left (built on the site of Dr. Gully's house), go out on to Priory Road. Turn right and at the far end of the car park turn left along Clarence Road and follow this down to just before the railway bridge, where a left turn will lead back to the station.

The Abbey Gate House Museum

2
Round North Hill

This walk involves a steep climb up on to the hill, followed by a walk around North Hill, giving views to east, then north and west.

> **Distance:** Nearly 4 miles (6.5 km) – a comfortable two hour walk.
> **Maps:** Landranger 150; Explorer 190.
> **Car Parking:** Several car parks in Great Malvern.
> **Public Transport:** Buses and trains to Great Malvern.
> **Start/Finish:** Great Malvern railway station (GR783457).
> **Refreshments:** Several possible sources of refreshment in the town.

WALK to the top of the main shopping street Church Street, and at the top turn right as far as Barclays Bank. Cross over, and by the Unicorn Inn, an ancient pub some of which dates from the sixteenth century, turn left on to St. Ann's Road. This climbs very steeply up and out of the town, away from the noise of traffic.

Beyond the last house on the right are the wooden sheds which were used to stable the donkeys. In Victorian times it was quite normal to ride up to the top of The Beacon on the back of a donkey. Donkeys could be hired from here until the beginning of World War II, and they certainly eased the agony of the ascent for many visitors. About 200 yards beyond the last house on the left, when the surfaced drive bends sharp left and a grassy track goes straight ahead, turn sharp

One of the many fine gas lamps to be seen in Malvern

right following the concrete arrow in the small stone wall, pointing to Ivy Scar.

This is a fairly horizontal path, undulating through the tree covered hillside. At a fork in the path, the right fork goes downhill, but take the left to ascend slightly. Shortly a path comes up from the right to join us, and just continue along the broad stony track round to Ivy Scar rock on the left of the path, and a simple bench seat if you need a rest.

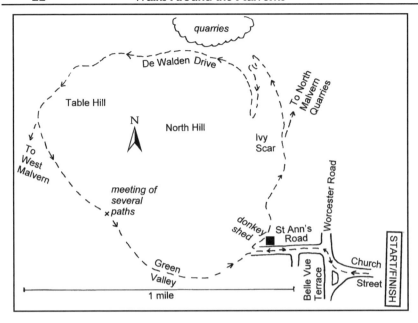

Ivy Scar is known as the largest natural rock outcrop anywhere on the hills. The rocks are part of an igneous intrusion of dolerite, and are younger than the surrounding rocks into which they were intruded. Several small plants have colonised these rocks, notably lichens which can grow on bare rock. In the cracks there are numerous succulent plants, wall pennywort (*Umbilicus rupestris*) which flower from June to August.

A few yards past Ivy Scar, leave the main track and fork left to go uphill along a narrow stony path. This leads on up to the open hillside, with magnificent views over Malvern Link, and across to Madresfield and Worcester. When the path has a sharp left elbow turn, look down and directly behind the spire of Madresfield church is the tree lined avenue of Madresfield Park. Ignoring a minor path right, our path soon has a right elbow turn, and then another to the left and continues on up to a T junction with a main driveway.

Turn right here along the Lady Howard de Walden driveway, which was built as a carriageway in the 1890s, having been financed by Lady de Walden who would occasionally drive on it around North Hill. The highest point on this drive is at 1125 ft (343m).

After a short distance the driveway narrows to a footpath and climbs slightly. This is because the original route, visible just down to the right, was interrupted by quarry workings and so a diversion has been essential. Further down to the right can be seen the Tank Clock Tower (walked past in Walk 6) erected in 1901 by the Urban Council.

The path goes above the top of the sheer 125m. face of Scar Quarry, one of the two North Malvern Quarries. From here is a very clear view not only of the straight line of trees in Madresfield Park, but also of the straight line of the main railway running from Malvern towards Worcester.

Once beyond the top of the quarry, the path descends slightly to rejoin the old route, as the former driveway comes in from the right. Walk on along this delightful track around the head of a deep green valley down to the right. Originally created by a river, it is likely that this valley was deepened by ice during the last glacial phase of the Ice Age.

Where the main path comes up from this valley, there is also a clear path to the left which leads over the col between Table Hill and North Hill, but just keep straight ahead, with End Hill over to the right. The track soon begins to bend round to the left, and views over Herefordshire open up. When walking due west the steep hill just south of Hay-on-Wye is often visible.

The track begins to descend towards West Malvern and bends further left until heading southwards. Paths come up from the right to join this track and shortly beyond this, is a seat 'In loving memory of Henry Egerton Chesney 1885-1973'. The track soon splits, to left and right of a lump of Malvern granite. The right fork descends to West Malvern, but fork left and go slightly uphill between a small quarry on the left, and a bench seat to the right. Look down on West Malvern, the school and the church. The main building in the school was the grand house built by Lady de Walden. In the distance to the south is the outline of British Camp with the Eastnor Obelisk to the right.

Climb gently up to a meeting of several paths shortly beyond a small overgrown gravel working on the left. Like a miniature Piccadilly Circus, routes go in all directions from here – including up to the Worcestershire Beacon away to the right, and North Hill to the left.

For a longer walk you can link up here with walk 3 (★ on page 25).

Our route is straight ahead and downhill, crossing over the main broad stony path, used by countless thousands on their way up to The Beacon.

Descend into the large valley – called Green Valley or Happy Valley, passing an arrow signpost in the small rocky wall, pointing to Great Malvern. The valley is lined with an avenue of sycamores, planted in the 1930s. Notice the change of climate in this valley. On a hot sunny day there is cool and refreshing shade here, but on a cold windy day, there is pleasant warming shelter. This leads straight down to St. Ann's Road, passing the source of a small stream on the right, which flows alongside the path. There are signs of paving stones beneath the grass in places, and these are the remnants of a former route from West Malvern.

The descent becomes steeper and steeper, to test out muscles not previously used on this walk – knees and backs of thighs. At the beginning of the surfaced drive, you can either go straight on and return by the way you came up, or fork right to St. Ann's Well, where you can get a drink from the spring or the café. There is plenty of opportunity for refreshment in Great Malvern if you carry on straight ahead to retrace steps down into the town, and then to the car park, or the station, wherever you started from.

Looking across Happy Valley towards the Worcestershire Beacon

3

A Spring Walk

Malvern is famous for its hills and its water, and this walk samples the delights of both.

Distance: 8 miles (13 km).
Maps: Landranger 150; Explorer 190.
Car Parking: Several car parks in Great Malvern.
Public Transport: Buses and trains to Great Malvern.
Start/Finish: Great Malvern railway station (GR783457).
Refreshments: Several possible sources of refreshment in Great Malvern; and the Wyche Inn at the Wyche Cutting (on the Worcestershire side).

STARTING from the station in Great Malvern proceed up hill along Church Street the main shopping street, and at the top on the opposite side of Belle Vue Terrace is the Robson Ward Furniture shop. In its entrance courtyard is the Bottling Works spring, simply a hole in the wall nowadays.

On leaving the location of the old bottling works, turn left, and then left again to ascend the very steep hill of St.Ann's Road. When the surfaced road ends, just keep straight on up the beautiful tree lined pathway into Green (or Happy) Valley, with a stream on the left side of the path. Pass the source of this stream and keep climbing, branching left as you approach the highest point.

At the major track which crosses this path, turn left, following the signpost to The Beacon.

★ *If you are combining walks 2 and 3 join here from walk 2. Turn right, following the signpost to The Beacon.*

The track is now fairly level and will lead on to a major crosspaths with a round stone route indicator. Turn right here towards the Dingle and West Malvern. After 25 yards the broad path splits and you take the left fork, going round the side of the Dingle, with views down to the right where several houses are tucked snugly in the valley. Bend left round the side of the hill, with the Worcestershire Beacon up to your left as you follow the gentle route along the west side of the range.

After about 350 yards fork left on a narrower ascending path. The path then becomes fairly level, passing a seat and a walled garden, and down to the right is the West Malvern road B4232. Keep straight along the path until it reaches a broad parking space alongside the stony road which links the car parking areas. The way ahead is 30-40 yards across the parking space which then narrows down to a footpath. But before proceeding along this turn right and descend through a few pine trees to the road in order to visit the Hay Slad Spout, one of the most powerful of the Malvern springs.

Alongside the road, Hay Slad Spout is a very popular spot for bottle fillers. Its easy access by car, and a very reliable flow, even in dry spells, encourages regular visitors to come here with their water bottles. Local water authorities recommend boiling this water before drinking, but many of the regulars do not take notice of this advice.

After visiting this fast flowing source of water retrace your steps up to the footpath which leads through trees, with the car park down to the right. As the path widens out again, on the left will be seen the largest of the West Malvern quarries. This is a huge amphitheatre, with trees clinging to the steep rocky slopes (see Walk 7).

On leaving the quarry turn left up the slope on to a flat grassy path and walk into the woods at the far end of the grass. The broad path leads to a gradual climb up to the main path on the ridge top which is quite low at this point. At another Indicator Stone (the Gold Mine) turn right to walk down to the Wyche Cutting.

Cross over the road and climb the steps alongside the bus shelter, to continue walking southwards, following the signpost 'Hill Top Walk to British Camp'. There are two paths along the ridge top, the right side giving better views over the undulations of Herefordshire and the left side looking across the plain of Worcestershire. Go over (or around) this hill top and down the other side, then up the next rise, with fir trees on the right. The hill is now named Jubilee Hill to celebrate the Golden Jubilee in 2002. A stone at the top was unveiled by HRH the Duke of York. Go ahead and descend again, but before starting to climb Pinnacle Hill turn sharp left past the memorial seat to A and M E Edmonds. The path steadily descends through deciduous woodland. Reach another path and turn sharp right, still descending. After being joined by a path from the left emerge to a splendid view over a deep valley at the bottom of which is the Holy Well. At the top of the valley up to the right is the bare hill top of Pinnacle Hill, a location popular with hang gliders.

Follow the path round the head of the valley and keep left at an iron seat when the path splits, with the right fork going uphill. To the right and about 50 yards along this path is a tiny pond, no more than a puddle nowadays. This is the Eye Well, dating from 1622 or even earlier, and famed for curing eye ailments, in the days of the water treatment. Beyond this, at a memorial seat, turn very sharp left to descend down the valley. Bluebells and wood sorrel are prolific here. As this path levels off turn right on a very steep zigzag path down to the buildings of the Holy Well.

This is located on the old coaching road, and in 1558 Queen Elizabeth granted this spring and surrounding land to John Hornyold who held the title of Duke of Gandolfi. Water has been bottled on this site since 1622, and Dr. Wall built the first bath house here in 1753. In the eighteenth century this was the most important well, but St. Ann's became more popular after 1823. A plaque on the wall commemorates the 150th anniversary of the Water Cure (in 1992).

From Holy Well turn immediately left along the broad and nearly horizontal track (signposted 'bridleway'). This leads through the woods nearly a mile back to the Wyche Cutting, on a path constructed in the eighteenth century. It is mostly horizontal and passes through woods rich in trees, flowers and birds, with many warblers here in the summer. Pass the simple fence on the right which borders the grounds of the Cottage in the Woods Hotel and fork left here, slightly uphill, when the track divides. Emerge at the road by a few houses, and go straight ahead and steeply down the Old Wyche Road. Just to the left is the new Wyche Road and the Wyche Inn.

The Wyche Cutting takes its name from wic or wych, the old English name

The Holy Well

for salt, and it was on the old packhorse route or saltway from the River Severn to Hereford. The cutting is along the line of a geological fault, and at a height of 261m (856 ft). The existing road cutting was made in 1840, and widened at the beginning of the twentieth century. The cottages near to the Wyche were mostly built for railway workers and quarrymen in the nineteenth century.

Another Victorian gas lamp

The Old Wyche Road is a very steep descent, and must have been a hard climb for the horse drawn vehicles and the early travellers. As the road levels off, beyond the junction with Lower Wyche Road, the Lower Wyche Spout is on the grassy patch to the left of the road. This emerges through a stone and brick wall, and trickles down to a drinking trough nearer the road. The inscription is well weathered but mentions that it was erected for the accommodation of the local inhabitants by Charles Morris in 1840.

Walk up to the top of this grassy area and turn right along Lower Wyche Road. A good view of Malvern Common below can be seen, and soon on the left of the road is the delightful old stone building of number 10, Spring

The Girl's College, formerly the Imperial Hotal

Cottage: on the road near to its gate is another spring beneath a grating on the edge of the road. Further along Lower Wyche road, just before it joins the main Wyche road, is yet another spring on the left which feeds an animal drinking trough.

At the main road turn left, and after about 100 yards, cross over the road to a footpath. Ignore the left fork to the Wyche Cutting, but continue forward towards St.Ann's Well, passing the seat in memory of Con and Lena. All over the hills there are convenient seats, many of which are memorials to those who have enjoyed walking the Malverns.

After a slight climb, with the road down to the right, the path levels and becomes an easy walk northwards. Then at cross paths there is a sharp left turn uphill, or a right turn downhill, but we just keep straight ahead. This leads us on through the trees to a steep valley, called Rushy Valley, a very sheltered valley rich in trees and birds.

From the bench seat here there are excellent views over the town, with the main building of the Girls College being prominent. Up to the left at the top of this rock strewn valley, is the Dripping Well, at a height of 310m (1020 ft), one of the highest springs on the hills, and it generally keeps flowing even through dry spells of weather. On different occasions I have seen a kestrel, a stonechat and a robin bathing in this pool.

Continue on to St. Ann's Well (*see walk 1*) and take the surfaced right-hand track. This zigzags steeply down to reach a road. Turn right here, then almost immediately left along a driveway signed 'Half Way'. Then, to the left of entrance gates, go down 95 steps (traditionally known as the 99 steps), back into the town centre and to your starting point.

Priory Church as seen from the bottom of the '99' steps

4

Back from Colwall Station

A short railway trip through the tunnel beneath the Malvern Hills to Colwall, followed by an exhilarating walk along the Malvern ridge back into Great Malvern.

Distance: Nearly 7 miles (11 km).
Maps: Landranger 150; Explorer 190.
Public Transport: Train to Colwall.
Start: Colwall ralway station.
Finish: Great Malvern.
Refreshments: Malvern Hills Hotel and a snack bar at Wynds Point; Wyche Inn at the Wyche Cutting.

ATCH the train in Malvern for the regular service to Ledbury and Hereford, and take the five minute journey to Colwall. This involves passing through the tunnel beneath the hills. The original tunnel was built from 1853-1861, and was very slow work, cutting through the hard rocks. Because parts of the tunnel were crumbling, it was closed in the early 1920s, and a new tunnel was built alongside it. This was opened in August 1926, having taken two and a half years to complete, and with a length of about 1500 yards. Much of the rock cut through is syenite, and the spoil dug out to make the second tunnel had just been left lying around, but was used as road metal in the construction of part of the M50 – a good piece of conservation.

Cross over the footbridge to leave the station, and from the bridge is the first of several superb views of the Herefordshire Beacon. Pass to the left of the small pond, and go through a small kissing gate into a field. Walk up the left margin of this field, a real traditional untreated meadow, with wild flowers and grasses.

At the top of this field, go over the stile and straight on for a few yards, then bend slightly right and climb steeply up the slope. *Do not turn right into the narrow strip of woodland.* Follow the yellow arrow and soon emerge through the trees into a meadow. Walk along the top edge of the woods for about 50 yards, and then turn left straight up the field. At the top of this field, pass over a stile into a green track between a hedge and a line of trees. Ignore a waymarked stile which goes left, and at the top of this field turn right following the fence to the end of the field where there is a stile.

Climb over this stile and then turn right and go downhill through the woods, then swing left over another stile and into a grassy field. The path gradually moves over to the right margin of the field, leading on to a kissing gate and into the next field. Go along the right margin of this field for almost 100 yards, then over the stile into the woods and immediately turn left to follow a clear path. This is a bluebell wood with rich bird life, as well as flowers and a variety of trees. The path leads through to a stile and then down to the driveway of Spindrift.

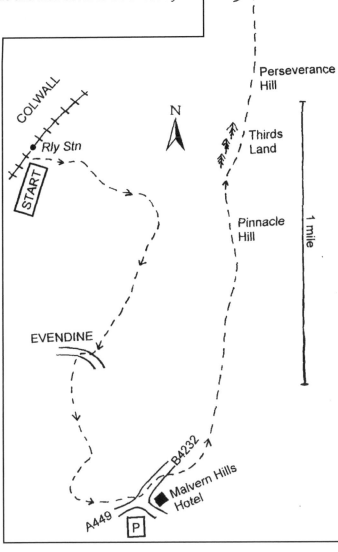

To next page

tunnel

Perseverance
Hill

N

Thirds
Land

Rly Stn

START

COLWALL

Pinnacle
Hill

1 mile

EVENDINE

B4232

Malvern Hills
Hotel

A449

P

Follow this drive, over a small ford and out on to the minor road (where there is a convenient seat) in the small hamlet of Evendine.

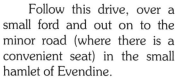

Turn right here for about 50 yards and then left just past Upper House, to walk along the edge of the garden. This path leads on over a stile and across a field, swinging half left when you meet a hedge and continue forward when you leave it. At the end of the field go over the stile and across a footbridge, then across another field towards a stile.

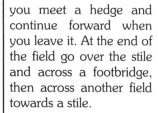

If you are using part of this walk to reach Wynds Point for walks 9, 10 or 11 you can at this stage take a short cut. Cross the stile and continue straight on, climbing to Wynds Point.

For the main walk turn right just before reaching this stile to walk alongside the hedge. Turn left at the end of the field, go over a stile and climb slightly, with a fence on the left and a hedge on the right. This passes on the right an outcrop of limestone from the Silurian period, with many small fossils.

At the top of this stretch, turn left over a stile, signposted to British Camp and car park, and go straight on along the left edge of a narrow strip of woodland. Go over another stile and on up through the woods, with the noise of traffic increasing. This leads up quite steeply to the Wynds, with the toilets, Malvern Hills Hotel and a snack bar awaiting you if you feel like some refreshment.

Turn left along the West Malvern road (the hotel on your right), and after about 250 yards, at the grassy car parking area, fork right up on to the hill, to walk the two miles to the Wyche. There is a path along the ridge top, with excellent views over Worcestershire and Herefordshire. There is a slightly lower path on the west side if preferred, which gives good views over

Herefordshire, though not Worcestershire, and is generally more sheltered from the wind.

The highest peak along the ridge is Pinnacle Hill, reaching 357m (1171 ft). There was formerly a shelter on this hill, but in 1826 lightning killed several people sheltering in it, and it was removed. Near this summit, in a slight hollow, are the remains of two tumuli, dating from about 1000BC, the Bronze Age. Just beyond Pinnacle Hill is the top of the fir plantation called Thirds Land, on the western slopes. Here there are larch and pine planted in the nineteenth century – the only large coniferous area on the Malvern Hills.

Looking north towards Pinnacle Hill

From the top of the ridge you can see the Three Counties Showground site, and just to the right of this is a straight hedge marking the line of the old branch railway from Malvern Wells to Tewkesbury, which was open from 1864-1952. The fields near this old railway route are large and rectangular, as the result of reclamation and enclosure of common land. Where the railway cuts diagonally across these, small triangular fields were created alongside the line. To the right of Thirds Land the hill was named Jubilee Hill in 2002, and there is a memorial stone unveiled by the Duke of York. Continue beyond here, over Perseverance Hill, and then descend towards the Wyche.

At the Wyche Cutting (*see Walk 3*), descend the steps and cross over the road, with the cutting to your right. Go about ten yards along the West Malvern road, before forking right up Beacon Road. Follow this narrow surfaced road gradually uphill, passing a car park on the left and then another on the right. Cross the line beyond which no cars are allowed, even though it is still surfaced.

From the round indicator stone, at the point known as the Gold Mine, follow the arrow pointing north-east to the Quarry Walk, St. Ann's Well via Earnslaw. Earnslaw is an old quarry which now contains a lake, and is popular with walkers and picnickers. It has been stocked with fish by the Conservators, though no fishing is allowed, and is surrounded by steep and dangerous slopes. Many interesting shrubs grow in this area, including buddleia and valerian, which have spread from a nearby garden.

Walk into the woods passsing a few tall sweet chestnut, and the path becomes narrow and stony, with a small boundary wall to the right, beyond which is a steep slope down hill. The path descends slightly and the Earnslaw quarry is to the left.

Soon joined by paths from the right, our route emerges into an open grassy area, with steps up to a viewpoint over the quarry and lake on the left, and a few yards further on a pathway down to the lake, but our route is to the right, to descend a broad stony path.

Follow this path as it leads through woods down to the road. Just before reaching the road, as views open out over Malvern, the spire of the Christ Church and the main building of the Girls College, the old Imperial Hotel, can be seen straight ahead. Down at the Malvern-Wyche Cutting road, cross over and turn left.

Continue along this road (B4218) until it joins the A449. Turn left here and after about 50 yards go up some steps on the left (opposite the former Emmanuel Church), turn right and walk parallel with the road along a path that will take you into Rose Bank Gardens. Here you can go left to explore the gardens or continue forward along the lower path. Leave the gardens by the Mount Pleasant Hotel and Belle Vue Terrace is ahead of you. From here you can return to the station or other starting point.

5

The Malvern Hills Ridge Walk.

Taking you along the full length of the ridge from south to north this is the most strenuous walk in this collection. There are some steep slopes and more than 1000 m. of climbing but you will have magnificent views over Worcestershire and Herefordshire and an opportunity to scale all the Malvern peaks.

Distance: 10 miles (16 km); or 13½ miles (21.5 km) if starting from Eastnor, 16 miles (25.5 km) if starting from Ledbury.
Maps: Landranger 150; Explorer 190.
Starting Points and Transport: Ideally, two cars or a chauffeur are necessary for this walk, as public transport is very limited in the southern hills. If you can be dropped off at the southern end (Chase End Hill, GR757349) or leave one car there with another waiting at the northern end, then the problem will be solved. In this case start reading from ❋ on page 37.
For a rather longer walk you may like to be dropped off at Eastnor Park (GR737373), in which case start reading from ✪ below.
If neither of these options is possible you can use public transport by taking the train or the bus from Malvern to Ledbury (GR708387), then walking to the southern edge of Chase End Hill. This will involve an additional six miles.
Refreshments: Malvern Hills Hotel and a snack bar at Wynds Point; Wyche Inn at the Wyche Cutting; pubs, cafés and restaurants in Great Malvern.

IF you are starting from Ledbury follow the directions for Walk 15 as far as Eastnor. At the village school turn left and walk to the main road. Turn right there, and go along the road for about 400 yards before turning into Eastnor Park.

✪Follow the horizontal driveway to reach the large grassy area used as a caravan site, looking out for two small lakes over to the left. When you are level with the start of the second lake turn right along a rutted track to walk up the slope to the Obelisk. Continue straight ahead, passing the Obelisk on your right, and a broad track leads to a gate and a kissing gate at the edge of the Eastnor Estate.

Once through the kissing gate turn right on the track along the side of Midsummer Hill. This gives a quick route through to Hollybush and the main road A438. The track climbs at first, then descends slowly, passing a house (Castle Copse Cottage) on the way.

Cross the A438 and turn right, to walk past the bus shelter (where the pavement ends) and after another 40 yards turn left through a gate, into the woods. The path immediately splits, but take the right fork, climbing quite steeply to join a broad path, and turn right along this. Follow this fairly horizontal path along the side of Raggedstone Hill and through to the small hamlet of Whiteleaved Oak. The walk is mostly through woods, but to the left are some patches of bracken and gaps in the trees on the slopes of Raggedstone. The path through the woods passes a small spring on the left, and then gradually slopes down, in what is often a muddy stretch, to pass between two houses, through an old iron gate and out on to a track.

Turn left here, passing a couple of the delightful old houses of Whiteleaved Oak, and at the road turn right. Walk past a small post box on the right and continue along this country road for three quarters of a mile. Up to the left the triangulation point on Chase End Hill may be seen. This road passes through

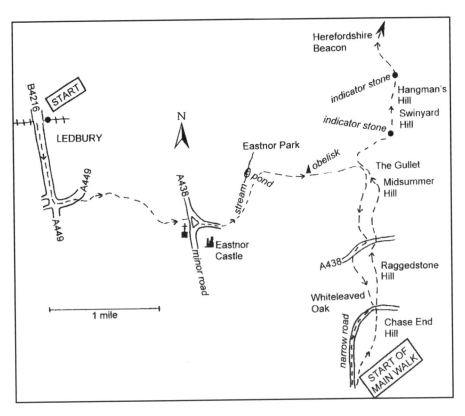

beautiful Herefordshire countryside, with masses of wild flowers in the spring. Just past the point where a footpath comes in from the right is the fairly isolated Hill House and further on is a brick built house called Fernlea. A few yards beyond this is the real starting point of the ridge walk, and a small area available for road side parking.

❋ Here begins one of the finest ridge walks in England, and on a clear day the views are magnificent across Herefordshire and Worcestershire, and beyond. The views are often surprising as this ridge gives an impression of great height, in spite of nowhere going above 425m.

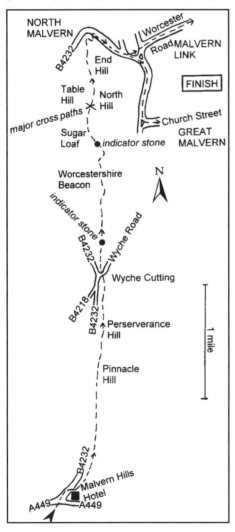

On the side of the road opposite Fern Lea ignore a stile leading into a field but take the signed path to the left of this leading into woodland passing a concrete name sign of Chase End Hill set in the middle of a block of local rock. After about 50 yards the path splits at a wooden post with two yellow arrows. Follow the broader path to the right, but where this goes straight ahead through a gate and into the woods, ignore that option, and bend left to follow the clear path which leads steadily up to the summit of Chase End Hill.

Views begin to open out before reaching the top, and there may be noise of the M50 away to the south. Throughout the length of the walk there will be occasional noises drifting up from the plain below, which seem very remote and often unreal on the exposed windy world of the ridge top. This path to the summit is quite worn, one of many very well worn paths in the Malvern Hills.

Chase End Hill is at the junction of Gloucestershire, Worcestershire and Herefordshire and is located at the southern end of the Malvern Chase, which was the Royal Forest (see *Walk 13*).

The view ahead shows the Eastnor Obelisk and to the right of that are the twin peaks of Raggedstone Hill, the second of the Malvern ridge summits. We are heading to the left hand peak of the two, via Whiteleaved Oak, surely one of England's most picturesque hamlets, with delightful old houses and gardens, one of which is still well terraced.

The path ahead from the trig point splits, but take the left fork to descend very steeply down a grassy slope, and straight on to a path leading past Cider Mill Cottage (note the remains of a cider mill in the garden) to a hedged drive, and out on to the road in Whiteleaved Oak.

Turn right along the road, passing the post box on the left (which you will have seen before if you have walked from Eastnor), and bend right to follow the road for about 30 yards. Fork left along a track, passing a bungalow on the right and then go through a wooden gate, the beginning of Malvern Hills Conservators territory. Pass another house on the right and just beyond the gate and garage of this house, turn left to leave the track and take an easily missed narrow path going uphill between bracken and gorse.

This is a steep climb up through the trees. There are tree roots on the path and higher up it becomes quite stony, as the path emerges above the trees and through the final gorse bushes to the open hill top. Here is one of the best parts of the Red Earl's Dyke cut out of solid rock near the top of this climb (see *Walk 13*).

We have now reached the left summit of Raggedstone and the other peak is across a small valley about 100 yards to the right. Walk straight ahead to the end of the summit ridge, and see the views of the Obelisk, the Hollybush

The line of the Red Earl's Dyke on Raggedstone Hill

quarries and the top of Midsummer Hill, the next peak on this walk, with a small shelter visible near the summit.

At the end of the ridge ignore the clearer path leading straight ahead but fork left across the grass and moss to a path going through the bracken. This is somewhat indistinct in places but eventually leads down to a clear path which runs round the lower slopes of the hill. Turn right for a few yards and then soon go left down to the gate and the road. Turn right along the road, pass the wooden bus shelter (good for a picnic in cold or wet weather) and then cross over into a small parking space. Ignore the stony track along the left (west) side of the hill: our route is straight up the grassy slope and into the woods. This steep climb leads through bushes at first and then up into the trees. A clear path can be seen and when it splits either route will lead on up, but take the right fork to give a good view over the top of one of the Hollybush Quarries. The path emerges above the trees and Eastnor Obelisk is prominent to the left. The higher bare part of the hill has grasses and moss, with many outcrops of bare rock. To the left there is bracken and then trees lower down, but on the right is a larger expanse of woodland.

At the National Trust sign for Midsummer Hill is the largest embankment of the Iron Age fort. Go on over this and out on to the summit ridge where a small concrete shelter is located. The plaque inside tells that it was given to the National Trust in 1923 in memory of Capt. Reginald Somers Cocks MC.

The main part of the Iron Age fort is down to the right in the trees, but our route is straight ahead, and then down through the embankment and following the path which bends round to the left. The Gullet quarry can be seen over to the right, with Swinyard Hill beyond and Castlemorton Common to the right of it. The path passes a field on the right with a small stone and brick house tucked away in the hollow.

At the T-junction with a track, turn right and descend gradually to a major cross tracks. The right turn leads to The Gullet, the left goes through the gate into Eastnor Park, but we go straight on. The track leads into the woods, and the path can be muddy, although there is now a narrow path to the side of the track. After about 500 yards the track splits where the wood opens out very slightly and bracken can be seen. Our route is to the right, along a broad path which climbs slightly and emerges on to the open ridge by an easily missed Indicator Stone, with arrows north to British Camp, east to Castlemorton Common, the Gullet south and the Obelisk and Midsummer Hill back the way we have just come.

We continue northwards to British Camp by walking along the ridge top, which is often windy, and is sometimes used by hang gliders who can launch themselves out and descend to the lovely Castlemorton Common below. At the end of Swinyard Hill the path descends to a cross paths where a narrow gap is created at a major geological fault. Go straight ahead, ascending a worn path and after about 30 yards the path splits, with the right fork signed to Broad Down and Hangman Hill, but we take the left fork which is really straight ahead. Keeping to the main path this leads past the Giant's Cave and on to another indicator stone.

The arrows on this stone point back to Giant's Cave and Pink Cottage where we have just come from, to Hangman's, Shadybank and Broad Down over to the right, straight ahead Camp Hotel and Wynds Point, up to the left British Camp Earthworks, and this is the way we are going.

Just beyond the Indicator Stone is the line of the Red Earl's Dyke coming from the right and this continues parallel to the path we now follow.

The Giant's Cave (Clutter's Cave)

The man made crazy paving path of local stone ascends steeply. After passing the first embankment and ditch of the earthworks, the stone path ends and we enter the Iron Age camp via the South Gate (*see Walk 10*).

Go northwards along the grassy surface where huts existed about 2000BC. The views down to the left look out on two farms with a line of trees in between, and these trees mark the line of the old Ridgeway route (*see Walk 11*).

From the highest level of the Camp, the views can be quite spectacular, and looking north the worn path on the ridge top shows the next part of the walk. First we have to descend the stepped and surfaced path on the right to the car park and Wynds Pass, used by the main Tewkesbury to Ledbury road,

A449. Cross over this road, passing between the Malvern Hills Hotel and the snack bar, the first places to offer refreshment along this walk. The next opportunities are at the Wyche Cutting in two and a half miles, and these are the last along the route, until arriving in Malvern.

Cross over and walk left along the road to West Malvern, and immediately beyond the drive leading into the rear of Malvern Hills Hotel, walk up the steep path on the grass, and reach a grassy area with fine views looking north. This level path passes left of a wooden seat,then passes four more and a memorial to Sir Barry Jackson, Founder of the Birmingham Repertory Theatre and the Malvern Festival. Just before reaching the woods, turn left to pass on the right side of the impressive stone house.

Climb the first hill, and beyond this are several other undulations, with Black Hill first, and then Pinnacle Hill which is the highest. Where the fir trees are to the left, the next hill is Jubilee Hill, named in 2002 to celebrate the Queen's Golden Jubilee. The next hill is Perseverance (325m/1066 ft). and beyond this descend a few steps to reach the road at the Wyche Cutting. Toilets are to the left, and a pub to the right of the Cutting.

For the way ahead cross over the road and walk along Beacon Road, then immediately after passing cottages take the path on the right. Swing right to then walk left of a fence passing a ventilation shaft. Pass an indicator stone and keep along the path to the right of the tarmac track. When the gorse bushes on your left permit you can move over to slightly higher ground with a better view.

The path ascends, then drops down to rejoin the surfaced track – exposed to wind but with open views to east and west. Walk along this track for about 40 yards, then by a seat go straight ahead along the path to reach the summit of The Beacon.

Carry on from The Beacon, straight ahead and downwards by means of one of several of the paths which descend to a col below, where several paths meet at an indicator stone. The arrows on this point back to The Beacon, right to Horseshoe Bend, St. Ann's Well, Great Malvern, to the Dingle on the left, and to Sugar Loaf Hill which is the next hill on the ridge walk.

The main path goes straight ahead to North Hill but go slightly left here on the narrow path to make the small ascent of Sugar Loaf from where are good views left down to the Dingle Valley and to West Malvern. Down to the right is Happy Valley lined with trees.

After a short descent take the centre of three paths to reach a gap used by paths crossing the ridge from West to Great Malvern. Go slightly right of straight ahead and on up a grassy slope to the small col between Table Hill (373m.) on the left, and the much higher North Hill to the right. At the top of this col, detour right to the summit of North Hill (397m.), the second highest peak along the ridge and with fine views of Worcestershire.

Return to the col and then detour left to the summit of Table Hill for views from here of Herefordshire.

Now carry on down beyond the col to near the wooden bench on a broad horizontal path which is the Lady de Walden Way. Turn left and after just over 100 yards when this track bends left by another wooden bench, turn right down a steepish grassy patch heading towards End Hill, the last hill on the ridge. After the descent is a short steep climb from where there are excellent views northwards to the Abberley Hills. The top of End Hill has a few rocky outcrops, plus small rock fragments, looking similar old hard rock to what has been seen in several locations during this idge walk. End Hill is not quite the end as there are two small undulations before going down the final grassy slope to a track. Turn right along this, soon to bend right and descend between broom bushes. The track leads down to the trees, has a sharp left bend and then reaches the West Malvern Road.

Take great care here because of the traffic, but turn right and cross over to the pavement. Just before reaching the Clock Tower is the entrance to Tank Quarry picnic place, where a small geological display provides information about local rocks. Walk on to pass the Clock Tower, built by the urban council in 1901.

The inscription on the tower states:

> *The inhabitants of North Malvern have placed this stone to re...(weathered away) that these tanks were erected at the sole expence of Charles Morris Junr. Esq. of Portman Square London in 1835 and 1836.*

Just before reaching Holy Trinity church is a road which provides the shortest way to Malvern Link station for pedestrians, as it is a No Entry road for traffic. From this cross the B4503 and go left along the A449 to reach the station. Approaching the station look out for the fine Victorian post box.

To return to Great Malvern walk on between Holy Trinity Church on the left and the old pound, the stocks and whipping post on the right, and at the main road turn right along Worcester Road to walk into the centre of the town.

MALVERN LINK is the northern suburb of Great Malvern. Although it has a modern sound 'Link' is derived from 'Hlinc' which means 'lower slopes'

6

To North Hill

This walk of nearly four miles, giving some magnificent views, includes a long and fairly steep climb followed by a shorter but fairly steep descent.

Distance: Nearly 4 miles (6.5 km).
Maps: Landranger 150; Explorer 190.
Car Parking: Malvern Link Common.
Public Transport: Train to Malvern Link station.
Start/Finish: Malvern Link Common (GR783474).
Refreshments: The Morgan pub on the A449 in Malvern Link.

FROM the railway station or Malvern Link Common walk up the hill along the Worcester Road. On the left hand side is the Temperance Drinking Fountain, one of Malvern's many springs, though it is now dry. It was put up by members and friends of the British Women's Temperance Association in 1900. Nearly opposite, is one of Malvern's few surviving Victorian pillar boxes. Many of the trees along here are bedecked with mistletoe.

A little further up the road, is Alexandra Road, which is where Edward Elgar lived at Forli, number 37, from 1891-1899. Whilst living there, he wrote many of his most famous works, including the *Enigma Variations* and the *Imperial March*.

The Victorian pillar box

Where the main road bends left, go straight ahead and over the grassy patch, crossing the B4503 and Hornyold Road to reach the narrow one way street going uphill. Turn right along this and walk about 300 yards to the quarries and the Tank Clock Tower. Opposite the tower is the old Morris school, with a plaque on its wall, and just beyond the

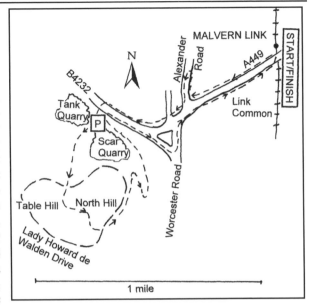

The Temperance Drinking Fountain

Tower is the Tank Quarry, closed in 1970 and now land-scaped and developed for use as a picnic site. The Tank Quarry, as well as the West of England Quarries, was used by the B.B.C. for filming an episode of Dr. Who, back in 1968. One of the large expo-sures of rock is used for abseiling instruction.

The notice on the tower tells you that 'This clock was erected in the first year of the reign of His Most Gracious Majesty King Edward VII, by the urban council, 1901.' A somewhat eroded plaque below records that the tanks (on which the clock tower was placed) were erected 1835-36.

Clock Tower at the Tank Quarry

Take the steps immediately to the right of the tower, and climb up steeply, on to a stony path, and soon getting views into the quarry to the right. When the path splits into two sets of steps, with a path in between them, take the left fork. They all end up at the same place, but the left steps will give good views over the quarry to the left, as well as out across the lower area to the east and south. The quarry to the left is Scar Quarry which closed in 1960, whereas Tank Quarry remained in use for a further ten years.

Climb up through the trees, rich in bird life, and going on beyond where the paths join, ascend into more open land with a few trees, grass, bracken and gorse, with a lot of loose rocks strewn on the surface. The path is rocky with grass, but gradually becomes less rocky as more height is gained. The skyline ahead is now visible, and North Hill is up to the left. At a lone, fractured ash tree, and a major cross paths, keep going straight ahead. The path narrows, and climbs up to a major horizontal track, which is the Lady Howard de Walden Way (*see Walk 2*) by a lone gnarled hawthorn and a lone simple bench. Good views from here look northwards over End Hill, the most northerly of the Malvern summits. Banks and ditches in this area are relics of sheep enclosures from the nineteenth century.

Go straight across the drive, and on up the grassy path towards a low col, between North Hill (397m) to the left, and Table Hill (373m) to the right. At the top of this col, turn left along the grassy path which leads direct to the top of North Hill. This is not much of a summit, but does have a tiny cairn, and provides impressive views out to the east, over Malvern and the Severn Valley.

Take the path going right (south), and heading straight towards the top of the Worcestershire Beacon, not that we are going there on this walk. Descend slightly, and after about 200 yards at a small rocky outcrop the path divides. It is really a small cross paths but the route straight ahead is not very clear. Turn left here and the grassy path will lead you down steeply over a grassy area popular with rabbits to the broad track of de Walden Drive.

At this drive turn left, and admire the wonderful views out to the right. There is a tremendous feeling of height walking along this path, with almost aerial views down to the town below. Pass a wooden bench, and just before the second wooden bench (where the drive swings left) fork right along a narrow path going downhill,signed to North Quarry. This narrow stony path leads down to Ivy Scar rocks, and at the first elbow bend on this descent you will notice the views over Malvern Link, and the Common down below.

At Ivy Scar, turn left along the broad gravelly horizontal track. This soon begins to descend and leads into the quarry at Tank Clock Tower. This is Scar Quarry which was closed in 1960 and all the old buildings removed and debris tidied up. Trees and grasses were then planted on the quarry floor and and also on the scree slopes and rocky faces. Part of the floor is now a popular car parking area.

The stone from the Tank and Scar quarries was used for building in Victorian times – though it was difficult to cut and shape. During the present century it became more important for road building when the rock was crushed into gravel size pieces.

The old stocks and whipping post

At the main road, turn right and walk down the right hand side. The pavement ends at a bus shelter but just keep going along the grass, beneath an avenue of lime trees, and the path will lead down to an old gas lamp post on the side of the road, and the iron fence to the right which helps to preserve the stocks and whipping post. The ivy covered wall behind the stocks is the boundary of the old sheep pound, used for keeping lost animals off the hills.

Cross over towards Holy Trinity church, but continue along the road until just before reaching the road junction, (Great Malvern to the right and Worcester to the left) take a small footpath at the end of the churchyard, cross over the main road A449 and turn left. This leads past the Morgan pub, with a fine collection of Morgan car memorabilia, and down the hill back to the starting point.

The Morgan car factory is located in Malvern Link, the company having been founded by H.F.S.Morgan in 1909. Large manufacturers were not interested in helping him develop his car, a three wheeler in those days, and so he went ahead on his own. The first four wheelers were produced in 1936, and the company is still producing the 1930s style cars. 150 workers are employed by the company which produces about fifteen cars a week and has orders for the next 5-6 years. Each car takes about four weeks to make, depending on the model (there are three different models), and every one is hand made.

The Morgan pub

Two walks from the West of England Quarries

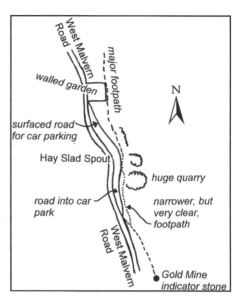

THE WEST OF ENGLAND Quarries are located on the western side of the Worcestershire Beacon, between the Wyche Cutting and West Malvern, on the B4232, and there is ample parking space in the old quarries. This is one of the highest parking places in the Malvern Hills, with the easiest access to The Beacon.

7

To The Beacon

This short walk climbs up from West Malvern Quarries to the summit of the highest point of the Malvern Hills. The Worcestershire Beacon reaches a height of 425m (1394ft), and has wonderful views all round Worcestershire to the east and Herefordshire to the west.

Distance: 2½ miles (4 km).
Maps: Landranger 150; Explorer 190.
Car Parking: In the old quarries on the West Malvern Road, near the Hay Slad Spout. Entry is possible from either the northern or southern end of the extended linear car parking areas. The main space is near the entrance at the northern end.
Public Transport: Service 675 between Great Malvern and Ledbury, Monday to Saturday.
Start/Finish: Car park GR 766448.
Refreshments: None available.

WALK SOUTHWARDS along the the stony driveway through the car parks, and go up to the higher quarry level near the southern end. Find the huge amphitheatre-like old quarry, the largest of the West

Malvern quarries and you will see some amazing plant colonisation, with trees growing high up the back wall, apparently out of the solid rock. It is mostly rowan, small elm and birch which colonise the steep slopes.

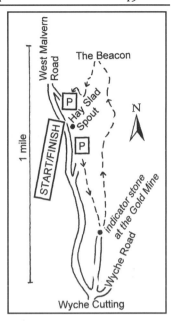

As you leave this quarry, turn left and follow the narrow path up out of the car parking area on to a flat area of grassland, where views over Herefordshire are superb. This western side of the Malverns is sunniest in the afternoons and summer evenings, and sunsets can be spectacular.

Cross this grassy area to a path at the far end, which leads into the woods. The path is fairly level, and then descends a little, to be joined by another path coming up from the right. From here, start to climb, ignore the right fork going downhill, and gradually emerge from the woods, to see stunning views over Herefordshire and across into Wales. Ranges of hills as far as the eye can see, undulating like waves on the sea.

The path leads up to the main ridge, at its lowest here (at 310m/1017 ft), and at the granite Indicator Stone, the surfaced track from Wyche Cutting to The Beacon will be reached. The Indicator is on the location of the Gold Mine, where a shaft was sunk from 1711-1721, in the search for gold and other minerals. It was known as the Gould Pitt in the seventeenth century. Small traces of mineral were found, but nothing of commercial value, even though the Malvern rocks have geological similarities to other rocks in which precious stones have been discovered. It was the flakes of shiny mica in the rock which made the early miners think they were about to discover gold. The marker stone points to Hay Slad, Wyche Cutting, Wyche Car parks, Quarry Walks and St. Ann's Well via Earnslaw, and The Beacon, which is the way we are going.

Follow the surfaced path (the M1 of the Malverns!) or the grassy or stony alternatives which all run more or less parallel to each other, and climb steadily up to The Beacon. Views over the Severn Plain or Herefordshire, or both, will be seen on the ascent, depending which path is followed. They all lead to the same place, the triangulation point and toposcope on the summit. Notice the trees only cover the lower slopes, and higher up the hill is quite bare, and is the reason for the name of Malvern.

The Beacon has been the location of many fires in the past, hence the name. The Beacon was lit at the time of the Spanish Armada, for Queen

Victoria's Jubilee in 1887, for Queen Elizabeth II in 1977, and most recently on the fiftieth anniversary of V.E.Day 1995.

There used to be a café at the summit, but it was burnt down in January 1989. Planning permission is unlikely to be given to build a replacement.

Also at the summit is the memorial to Queen Victoria's Diamond Jubilee in 1897. It is of granite, though not local Malvern granite. The wonderful views look over several counties, and the toposcope can name many of the visible landmarks. Every day is different, and something new can be revealed no matter how many times you walk to the top of this hill. It is a very prominent landscape feature, and if you were to travel due east from The Beacon, no land of comparable height would be reached until the Ural Mountains.

To descend, walk from the toposcope towards the trig point and turn right, i.e. to the west, and after 20-30 yards turn right along a broad stony path going slightly downhill. Ignore the sharp left turn after about 40 yards, (although this leads down to the West Malvern Quarries) walking north with the buildings of St. James's School in West Malvern ahead down at the foot of the hill.

After a further 50 yards, reach a simple wooden bench, turn sharp left and leave the broad stony path, to follow a narrow, but worn path going quite steeply downhill.

From this path is a magnificent view straight ahead to the Herefordshire Beacon, the Eastnor Obelisk and the charming village of Colwall down amongst the trees. Pass through the gorse and drop down towards the level of the trees and join a broad grassy path at a T junction and a seat, with a small stone wall behind it. These little stone walls built up by the Conservators are a splendid feature of many of the seats on the Malverns.

Turn right along the level grassy path, and after about 100 yards, sharp left at an elbow bend to go downhill. This leads down past old quarries on the left, and at the driveway through the parking area of the old quarries, turn right and walk back to the starting point.

You will notice the old quarries have been landscaped in places and many treees have been planted. The West of England quarries were bought by the Conservators in 1931, and many of the trees planted in the 1930s are now large and mature, especially the Austrian Pines which are over 60 years old.

8

Mathon

An undulating walk, crossing over ridges of Silurian limestone and valleys of Silurian shale. Several gentle hills to walk over and two very steep climbs on the return half of the walk. Starting from the very old Malvernian rocks, the walk crosses over the Silurian rocks which become younger moving westwards, although even the youngest, seen near Mathon, were formed more than 400 million years ago. There can be no finer scenery than this, anywhere in England, and the village of Mathon emphasises this with its name which is thought to be derived from an Old English word for treasure or gift.

Distance: 6 miles (9.5 km).
Maps: Landranger 150; Explorer 190.
Car Parking: At the northern end of the linear car park (GR766447) in the old quarries. Park on the largest part of this car park, not far from the pay and display meter.
Public Transport: See walk 7 (page 48).
Start/Finish: Car park at GR766447.
Refreshments: The Cliffe Arms in Mathon; two pubs in West Malvern.

WALK DOWN to the road (B4232) at the Hay Slad Spout, one of the most powerful springs on the hills. There are likely to be cars parked near the spring as many people come here to fill water bottles, and sometimes very large water containers. With your back to the spring, cross over the road and a few yards to the right is a clear footpath going diagonally downhill into the woods.

Pass a small brick building on the left and then the path narrows between hedge and fence, and good views open

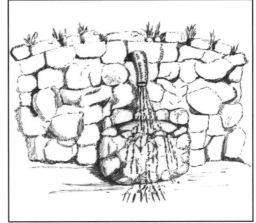

Hay Slad Spout

up to the west. Reach a track along which are a few fine houses, but go straight across between field and garden to continue descending along this bridleway. Reach the driveway of the modernised buildings of Park Farm, looking out for the old cider press on the right, and walk down to the road where there is an old fashioned Malvern style gas lamp.

Go left along the road for a few yards and then just before another old gas lamp, turn right to follow the yellow arrow through the gate with a notice saying: Private Road – Mathon Lodge Farm. After about 30 yards the drive splits, but keep left along the main stony drive, passing the iron gates of the Coach House on the left. Go over the stile and the path turns right and splits into two. Do not take the right hand possibility alongside the hedge, but the left fork which goes across the middle of the field to a gateway in the hedge at the far side.

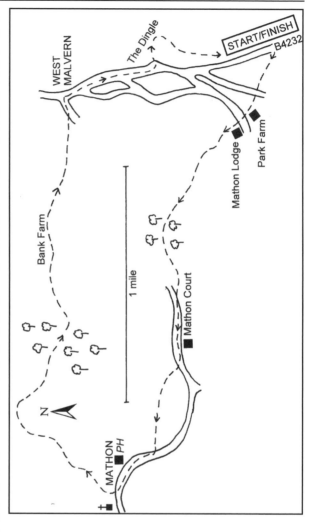

Climb over the wooden stile to the left of the iron gate and continue straight ahead along a path following an overgrown track between a fence and a hedge. To the left of the fence is a playing field. At the end of this stretch of path is another stile, beyond which a narrow path winds across the next field, slightly to the right of straight ahead. This field has been left as a field of grasses, wild flowers and trees. The path passes between trees on the way

Old cider press at Park Farm

across to a stile on the edge of the woods. Climb over this and follow the path through the mixed deciduous woods.

Leave the wood over the gate, and continue straight along a line of small hawthorn trees and through a gate beside an overgrown stile at the edge of the next field. Then go along the edge of another field, beneath a magnificent oak tree, and through a gateway and on to a track. This leads down to the road, and just before reaching the road is the driveway into Mathon Court.

Turn left along the road and walk past Rose Farm and then a house on the left just beyond which is a field containing a pond. Turn right here along a stony track. This leads past two black and white houses and beyond the second is a stile on the left. Go over this stile and follow the left margin of the field, soon with a stream on the left. Then go through a gate and across a small field.

Go over the next stile and follow the stream along the left margin of a larger field, to another stile and the road. Turn right along the road and walk into the village of Mathon, over the Cradley Brook, past the Cliffe Arms, several attractive houses and walk round as far as St. John the Baptist church. Next door to the church is the old school.

The red sandstone church has a large yew in the churchyard, and is often locked, but the key is available from neighbouring houses. Parts of the church date from Norman times, and there are interesting relics including a remarkable French seventeenth century painting of the flight into Egypt, and memorials to members of the Cliffe family, after whom the village pub was named. The ancient stone by the main door is where local people used to pay their tithes.

From the church retrace your steps, and 30 yards before the pub turn left over a stile and along a narrow path between gardens. Cross the footbridge and then turn right to follow the stony track which soon bends right and begins to climb, Keep straight ahead across a track, and notice the impressive buildings of Netherley Hall away to the left. When the track bends left towards the gate to Overley House, turn right over the stile and cross the small field to a stile in front of the old quarry. Climb over the stile and turn left on to the track. Pause in the quarry for a few minutes and search for fossils. You may find small shelly animals called brachiopods which lived in the Silurian period about 420 million years ago. Follow the stony track and pass to the right hand side of the house. Continue along the track to a pair of gate posts where a yellow footpath arrow indicates to go to the right on the grass. Bear diagonally across the flatter part of the field, with Netherley ahead and to the left. Near the far end of the field, go right and climb steeply up the hill and along the outside margin of the woods on Cockshot Hill.

At the top of this climb, go over the stile into the woods and follow the narrow path through to a broad track. Turn left along this track and continue through the woods, which are rich in wild flowers in spring. The track runs along the edge of the wood, with an open field to the right and Rowburrow Wood beyond. Views of the Malvern ridge open up straight ahead, with the Worcestershire Beacon and then the Herefordshire Beacon. At the end of the wood go through the gate, and turn left to go through another gate and follow the stony drive. Some of the stones on the drive are fossiliferous as this hill is built of Silurian limestone. Down to the right is a lush green valley.

Reach another gate, but just go straight on to Bank Farm and through the small hamlet to a narrow surfaced road. This leads down steeply to a valley where the rocks are softer shales, and then starts to climb steeply on to the next ridge of Silurian limestone. When the road bends right, the footpath goes straight ahead and into a small wood.

Emerging from the trees bear slightly right, as the path climbs up the grassy slope – another steep climb. Look for the marker posts with yellow arrow and pass to the right of a clump of trees half way up the slope in the middle of the field. At the top of the field is a stile leading to a small area of rough ground, and then another stile leading on a track through the farmyard of Croft Farm.

Walk along Croft Farm Drive and then left along Croft Bank, climbing uphill to West Malvern Road. On the right is part of St. James's School, and more of the school buildings are all around as you get on to West Malvern Road. Formerly St. James's, founded in 1902, this school amalgamated with The Abbey from Malvern Wells in 1979. The main school building is the magnificent house built in the1850s, and then enlarged on a grandiose scale by Lady Howard de Walden in 1890. The garden was also enlarged and at one time Lady de Walden employed 70 gardeners. Although she only lived in Malvern for ten years, Lady de Walden has certainly left her mark, with many buildings in West Malvern, her carriageway round North Hill and the money she provided for improving several hillside paths. She died in West Malvern in 1899, aged 92.

Mathon Church

Turn right along West Malvern Road to pass the church of St. James. In the graveyard is the grave of Peter Mark Roget, M.D., F.R.S. the writer of the famous, and still useful, *Thesaurus*. He died at West Malvern 12th September 1869, aged 90, whilst staying at Ashfield House where he spent many months during his later years. His grave is situated near to the War Memorial, and rather unusually lies in a north-south direction. The church itself is plain but does have fine east windows and a rather special brass altar rail. This was part of a rail formerly used in King Henry VII Chapel in Westminster Abbey, and was presented to this church in 1870 by the Dean and Chapter.

Beyond the church follow the road as far as The Dingle where the road widens and there is a parking area and a bus stop. At the far end of the parking area take the steep grassy path to the left, leading up alongside the houses which have been built in this deep and sheltered valley, reaching up to a height of 300m. This path joins the surfaced drive at the top of the houses, and continues uphill as a grassy track. After another 50 yards, turn right off this grassy track to join a stony track heading slightly downhill.

This broad path descends steadily through the woods. Where it splits, take either possibility. The left fork will lead to the top edge of the area of grass slightly uphill from the car parking area. The right fork will lead down to the road, and if you turn left along the road, past Radbrooke Lodge and Hillside, you will reach the car parking area.

Three walks from Wynds Point

THESE WALKS begin from the car park alongside the A449 where it cuts through the Malvern ridge, using a natural gap created by earth movements many million years ago. This gap was called Burstners Cross on some old maps, and was at the junction of several old tracks. The main stage coach route through the Malverns used this pass.

9

Little Malvern and Elgar's grave

A ramble into history, all on good footpaths and easily managed by families.

Distance: 4 miles (6.5 km).
Maps: Landranger 150; Explorer 190.
Car Parking: Beside the A449 (GR764404).
Public Transport: Bus service 675 from Great Malvern and Malvern Hills Hopper in the summer
Start/Finish: Car park at GR764404.
Refreshments: Malvern Hills Hotel and snack bar, both at Wynds.

START by crossing over the main road to walk along the B4232 West Malvern road with the Malvern Hills Hotel on the right. Once past the hotel driveway, fork right steeply up the grassy slope, to emerge, after passing a single seat, on to an open piece of grassland with several seats alongside the path. From the seats is a magnificent view looking north along the line of the hills, and up to the right behind the seats is an iron fence surrounding the garden of a house in which the famous Swedish singer Jenny Lind lived for a time. Known as the Swedish Nightingale, she lived there for the last 15 years of her life, and died in 1887, in her bedroom which faced out to the British Camp. She is buried in Great Malvern Cemetery and there is a memorial bust in the foyer of Malvern Theatres. The house is now owned by the Cadbury Trust and the gardens are occasionally opened to the public.

Between two seats is a memorial plaque to Sir Barry Vincent Jackson (1879-1961), founder of the Birmingham Repertory Theatre and the Malvern

Festival, Director of the Royal Shakespeare Memorial Theatre and the Covent Garden Opera Company. The quotation 'He nothing common did nor mean', is based on the writing of Andrew Marvell (1621-1678). The Festival was founded in 1929 and was an annual event until superseded by the creation of Malvern Theatres in 1998 with its wider and fuller programme.

The walk continues along the line of seats and then, ignoring a left fork, straight into the woods on a clear path. This rich deciduous woodland has carpets of bluebells in spring, other wild flowers and large numbers of birds, especially a variety of warblers in the summer. The path begins to descend and bends right and soon a sharp elbow turns to the left. The road is down to the right through the trees.

Ignore the next sharp elbow bend descending to the right and continue straight on a more or less horizontal path and round the head of a steep valley. Emerge from the trees to find superb views eastwards over the Severn Plain, with the top of Little Malvern Priory roof down below, and Bredon Hill and the Cotswold scarp beyond.

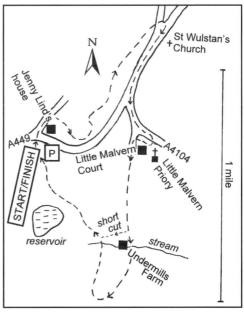

The woods are still to the left of this horizontal path but there is a cleared area to the right with bracken, which enables the views to be seen. Take a rest to admire the view on one of the many seats, the first of which is a memorial to John W. Roberts, Hills Ranger from 1954-1975. It is backed by a semi circular Malvern stone wall.

Continue northwards along the horizontal path. At a major cross paths take the right fork going downhill and keep on this as far as the road. Turn right on the minor road and after a few yards reach the main road. Cross over to the pavement and turn right, and walk on past the turning to Upper Welland.

Across on the right of the road is a Pine and Antiques shop, and on the left is St. Wulstan's Church. Before reaching the main door you will see the sign pointing to Elgar's grave, which is at the far end of the churchyard. Lady Elgar was buried here in 1920, then Sir Edward in the same grave in 1934. Their daughter Carice Elgar Blake was buried close to them in 1970.

After visiting the church, continue along the road and fork left on the A4104 to Upton, round to the Priory and Little Malvern Court. The Court and the magnificent gardens are open to the public from mid-April to mid-July, on Wednesdays and Thursdays from 2.15 to 5 p.m. There is an admission charge.

The Priory church next door is open every day and is free, and contains some very interesting relics. Its history dates back to AD1125 when a very small Benedictine monastery was built here. There were never more than about ten monks. The tower and small parts of the choir remain from the twelfth century. Ten monk's stalls can be seen in the present day church, but they have lost their misericords although some of the hand rests have survived. The misericords were probably destroyed by Cromwell's troops, and many of the stained glass windows have been destroyed. There are still a few interesting fragments of portraits of the Royal family remaining, including Edward Prince of Wales, who became Edward V. There is also Elizabeth Woodville, King Edward IV's Queen, but she is headless; and Princess Elizabeth who later became wife of Henry VII is on the next window together with her sisters Cecily, Anne and Katherine.

Little Malvern Court and Priory

On leaving the Priory retrace your steps a few yards along the road, and just past the Court turn left again along the bridleway. This leads alongside the topiary hedge of the Court and at the end of the gardens are lakes on the left. Just over half a mile along the track, and before reaching the Undermills Farm buildings sheltered down in the hollow, is a stile by a gate on the right. You can cut across this field and into the woods if you wish to save half a mile. If so, cross the field towards two large gates. Go through the left-hand gate and follow the narrow path through the woods, climbing steadily, with a small stream on the left. Reach a major track and turn right – now back on the route of the longer walk.

For the longer walk do not turn right over the stile but keep straight ahead. The surfaced track ends, but a stony and grass track continues. Go through a gate and into a field, and follow the grassy track along the right hand side of the field. At the end of the field is a small gate and beyond this is Shadybank Common.

Turn right once through the gate and climb to the top edge of the open common grazing area. At the top is a track where we turn right for the return journey to our starting point. This track begins to climb slightly and then more steeply into the woods, where the calls of green woodpeckers are likely to be heard. Descend slightly to cross a stream, where the path coming up from the right is the route of the short cut referred to earlier.

Cross the small bridge and continue alongside the stream, climbing up quite steeply to the side of the reservoir which dates from 1892. It was constructed to collect water from several springs, to supply Malvern with water – but is no longer adequate (though it has been brought back into service). The track alongside the reservoir leads back to the car park where we started.

The Malvern Hills Hotel

10

British Camp and Swinyard Hill

A walk over the exposed top of the Iron Age hill fort and along the ridge top before returning in the shelter of the woods on the western side of the hill.

Distance: 4 miles (6.5 km).
Maps: Landranger 150; Explorer 190.
Car Parking: See walk 9, page 56.
Public Transport: See walk 9, page 56.
Start/Finish: Wynds Point car park (GR764404).
Refreshments: See walk 9, page 56.

T O THE RIGHT of the entrance to the car park at Wynds Point is a surfaced path up to the top of the Herefordshire Beacon, known locally as The British Camp (see box on page 62). The path begins at the large Malvern Hills Conservators notice on the right where we walk through the wooden gate:

British Camp viewed from Pinnacle Hill

British Camp or Herefordshire Beacon, height 1115 feet. One of the finest earthworks in Britain, built about the second century BC, later enlarged and altered before the Roman conquest. It dominates the vicinity and commands magnificent panoramic views, esteemed by John Evelyn the diarist to be "one of the goodliest of vistas in England". The Red Earl's Dyke running along the crest of the hills was made by Gilbert de Clare, Earl of Gloucester, circa 1287, to mark the boundary between his territory and that of the Bishop of Hereford. At a spring nearby William Langland the famous fourteenth century poet "slombred in a sleping" and dreamt his "vision of Piers Plowman".

Thirty yards beyond the information board turn sharp right and then sharp left, gaining height rapidly along the surfaced path. Quickly emerging above the trees is likely to produce a change of climatic conditions, once the shelter of the trees on the lower slopes has been lost. Views open up over the reservoir and across the Severn Plain towards the Cotswolds.

Continue up to the first rampart of the old hill fort where the surfacing ends. Go forward and up steps to meet surfacing again. Now just keep going along this. This is one of only two areas in the Malverns where the path has been surfaced in this way, the other being the route up to the Worcestershire Beacon from the Wyche Cutting.

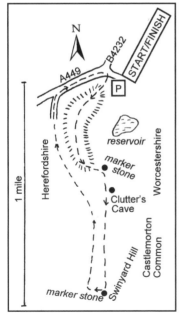

Ascend through more of the ramparts, and views open up into Herefordshire and across to Wales. At the summit (338m or 1111 ft), where the surfacing ends, pause and admire views all round, and notice that the range of Malverns to the north is slightly offset to the east, because of major faulting millions of years ago.

Walk on towards the south, descending, then ascending again, through the area where it is believed that most of the inhabitants of this fort had their houses when the summit was occupied. The climate is often very windy and exposed up here, and yet a settlement of up to 2000 lived here, and only wore rudimentary clothing. As you put on your sweater and anorak, try to picture conditions up here on a wet and windy day in February.

At the southern end of the summit ridge admire the view of the tree covered Ridgeway, Eastnor Obelisk and Eastnor Castle over to the right of the Obelisk,

British Camp: an Iron Age Hillfort on the Herefordshire Beacon

by Deborah Overton

The spectacular earthwork ramparts and ditches of an Iron Age hillfort encompass the whole of the Herefordshire Beacon and gives the hill its more popular name, British Camp. In prehistoric times the Malvern Hills with its many freshwater springs, might have always been a special and sacred place. British Camp was obviously built to impress, a demonstration of both power and status and although its appearance suggests a primary purpose as a defensive site, it could have had many other uses. This hillfort has not been positively dated but it is thought that the first phase of earthworks could date to the early Iron Age around 600BC, possibly even earlier into the late Bronze Age. Subsequent reworking of the ramparts around 400BC, expanded the enclosed area to about 12 hectares using the natural contours to include an outlying spur and a small summit to the south, recently named Millennium Hill. The earthworks extend for over a mile and a half and originally had four entrances set into the ramparts, three of which were contrived to face east with only one facing to the west.

A recent survey of the hillfort, undertaken by English Heritage (Bowden, M. with Field, D. and Winton, H.: *The Malvern Hills: An Ancient Landscape*, English Heritage 2005) identified the the circular platforms or bases for at least 118 buildings although it was not possible to say whether these were all in use at the same time. The buildings on these plots may have taken the form of roundhouses most of which were probably used as dwellings. Many of these sites had extended areas alongside them. These could have been yards or gardens or may have contained the four-post constructions similar to those found during excavations on the hilfort on Midsummer Hill, which were likely to have been used as stores, granaries and workshops. It has been suggested that up to 2000 people could have lived on British Camp and although this is possible, the hillfort may have been used only seasonally or during times of trouble or for specific rituals and celebrations.

The camp was possibly used in the Roman times although there is no evidence that Caractacus, the famous leader of the British, made his last stand here against the Romans.

During the early medieval period a Norman ringwork was constructed on the summit, both obliterating parts of and making use of the earlier Iron Age ramparts. This ringwork can be clearly seen for miles around and would have contained several buildings, some of which were excavated in the I 870s by Hilton Price. One of these building would probably have been a large timber tower which could have been used as a castle or later as a hunting lodge associated with Malvern Chase which was an important hunting ground belonging to the Earls of Gloucester.

before leaving through the South Gate to descend a steep path, made of lumps of Malvern granite. This can be a little slippery in wet weather. At the bottom of this slope is a round Indicator stone with arrows pointing to British Camp Earthworks, Broad Down, Shadybank Common, Hangmans Pink Cottage, Giant's Cave Pink Cottage.

Our route now swings right past Giant's Cave, also known as Clutter's Cave, a small man made cave in a large outcrop of basaltic rock. The origin is unknown but one story suggests it was occupied by a hermit– he certainly could not have been a giant as it is not large enough. Another legend suggests it was used by the fugitives John Oldcastle and Owen Glendower.

Continue straight on, with woods down to the right, and the bare hill to the left. Descend along a worn stony path to a meeting of paths, but keep straight on for another 30-40 yards to a meeting of five paths. This is at the bottom of the slope in a hollow known as Silurian Pass where a small outcrop of softer rocks occurs. Down to the right are some more of the softer rocks, mainly mudstones. These date from the Silurian period about 400 million years ago, and are much younger than the granites and gneisses of the Malvern Hills.

Go straight on and slightly uphill, following the small marker sign in the rock to the right of the path pointing to The Gullet and Midsummer Hill. The path leads up on to the ridge top of Swinyard Hill (272m or 895 ft), and as you proceed, views over Herefordshire and to the Eastnor Obelisk will be prominent ahead and to the right. Further along the ridge the views left over Castlemorton Common gradually open up. On many weekends, this is a popular location for hang gliders, who can just hang around, or float down to the Common below.

As the ridge descends towards The Gullet, another round marker stone will be reached on the right, with the arrows pointing towards British Camp, Castlemorton Common, Quarry Face no path, The Gullet, Obelisk Midsummer Hill. This is easily missed. If you find yourself going steeply downhill you have gone past it!

Clear views of both Midsummer Hill with its small hill fort and the Obelisk can be seen. Turn right following the path to Obelisk and Midsummer Hill, not that we are going to either of them today. The path soon enters the woods and at the T-junction a small wooden gate leads to the Obelisk. But we turn right along the track, now signed as the Three Choirs Way. The next mile is one of the few paths in the Malvern Hills area which often becomes muddy, because of the existence of the softer Silurian rocks.

We are now on the return journey, as we follow the track through the woods, with Swinyard Hill up to the right. Many birds and flowers can be heard or seen in these woods, and an abundance of wild garlic may be smelt in early summer. Ignore the path in a narrow gully overhung by trees, coming in from the right – this is the route from Silurian Pass – and just keep straight ahead.

At a cross paths, where a gate is to the left, keep straight ahead to an older gate and a stile. The stile has a yellow footpath arrow. Just beyond the gate on the right is Walm's Well, probably first used as long ago as 250BC. The covered reservoir on the left is used for storing water for the Eastnor Estate and village but has recently been investigated by Schweppes-Coca Cola as an additional source of supply. Follow the track through the woods to reach a major cross-tracks. Keep straight ahead, and climbing steadily we pass another cross-tracks and reach a recently cleared area of woodland on the left providing good views over Herefordshire. The woods on the right have a rich carpet of bluebells in the spring.

The track is very rutted, possibly because of vehicles coming for forestry work. At the top of the slope, before the track begins to descend, go right over a stile with a yellow arrow, to a footpath which soon becomes a track. Head out of the woods into a more open landscape. The Herefordshire Beacon is now up to the right. On reaching a house to the left join the stony drive and follow it down to the road. Turn left for 30 yards, with Beacon Lodge on the left and Allfields to the right. Turn right and follow the drive as it passes to the left of Allfields. As the drive bends right go left into the woods.

Descend along the clear path and reach a stile, then go out of the woods. Keep ahead along the left side of the field, and just before the next stile turn right, signed to British Camp car park. Go over the stile and follow the path into the woods, then climb steadily up to the old toilet block and the British Camp Hotel and Snack Bar.

11

The Obelisk Circuit

A walk to Eastnor passing the Obelisk, a prominent landmark that can be seen for many miles around.

Distance: 6 miles (10 km).
Maps: Landranger 150; Explorer 190.
Car Parking: See walk 9, page 56.
Public Transport: See walk 9, page 56.
Start/Finish: Wynds Point car park (GR764404).
Refreshments: See walk 9, page 56.

L EAVE THE CAR PARK along the path signposted to the British Camp and Broad Down in a stone sign embedded in the wall. After the first fairly gentle ascent, ignore the steep path going right, up some steps to The Beacon, unless you wish to go via the high point, but continue straight ahead, climbing gently. Views soon open out to the reservoir below, and across to the Cotswold scarp. On both sides of the path a few small patches of heather can be seen.

The broad gravel path leads to a round granite Indicator stone, where we turn left to follow the arrow east along a slightly sunken path towards Shadybank Common for 30-40 yards. At a tiny boundary stone with an indistinct letter L on it bend right to follow the elongated line of the Red Earl's Dyke leading southwards across Hangman's Hill. It is said that in medieval times criminals found hunting in the Royal Forest were hanged here.

Red Earl's Dyke is also known as Shire Ditch, and was dug between 1287-1291. It extends from the northern side of the Worcestershire Beacon as far south as Raggedstone Hill. It was named after the red headed Gilbert de Clare, the 7th Earl of Gloucester who had a dispute with the Bishop of Hereford about their territorial boundaries, and he built an embankment to clearly mark the limits of his hunting territory. It was designed by the Red Earl on the Worcestershire side of the summit ridge to enable deer from the Bishop's side to leap over into Worcestershire, but very difficult for the Earl's deer to leap over to the west.

Hangman's is a broad open grassy area, with trees growing on the slopes to right and left. Ahead can be seen Swinyard Hill, also with woods on both sides, and the Eastnor Obelisk prominent, away to the right. As the path descends, passing another marker stone it bends round to the right, still

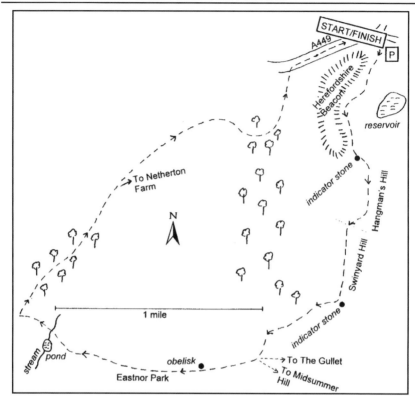

following the Red Earls Dyke. Swinyard Hill is clearly seen with Castlemorton Common down to the left.

The path leads down to a T junction with a broad stony path. Turn slightly left here along the stony path, not sharp left along the grassy path, and continue on downhill. At the bottom of the slope is a fiveway junction of paths. Go forward (signed The Gullet, Midsummer Hill) and up on to the ridge of Swinyard Hill (heading straight towards the obelisk which is about a mile away). Once up on the ridge top the obelisk will come into view through the trees, though the route is not straight towards it.

At the highest point of this hill, views over Castlemorton Common open up and there may be hang gliders taking off from the ridge top. Midsummer Hill is ahead, with woods covering the left, eastern slopes, and the hill fort being seen at the highest point. This is much smaller than the iron age encampment on the British Camp, but is well documented (*see Walk 12*).

The summit ridge begins to descend, and at the Indicator stone (*watch out carefully for this; it is easy to miss. If you find yourself still walking forward but starting to go steeply downhill you have missed it!*), turn right to follow the arrow pointing towards Midsummer Hill and the Obelisk. This path leads into the woods and at the T junction turn left through a small wooden gate by a cattle-grid, along the track, which often becomes muddy. Walk through the woods for 500-600 yards (ignoring a gate and stile on the right after about 400 yards) to a major cross tracks, where the route comes up from the Gullet to the left, and straight ahead leads to Midsummer Hill.

Turn right through the kissing gate with its notice saying Eastnor Park S.S.S.I. – no mountain bikes. Once through the gate, there are four paths to choose from – all very well worn. Take the second from the left (third from the right) and on the steady climb, there are good views left, up to Midsummer Hill, and down into the valley, where the remains of Bronsil Castle, home of Lord Beauchamp Lord Treasurer to Henry VI, are hidden by trees.

The path leads straight to the 90ft. high Obelisk on its grassy hilltop (240m) of Llandovery sandstone. The inscription on all four sides is quite worn by weather, and age. It is a family memorial erected in 1812, to The Honourable Edward Charles Cocks, elder son of John Somers, Lord Somers and Margaret, Lady Somers his wife, who died at Burgos in the Peninsular War. Another inscription on the side of the obelisk is memorial to Lord John Somers who was Lord High Chancellor of England in the time of William III.

Beyond the Obelisk go straight on (west) across grassy patches and through bushes and trees. Do not veer over to the left, where a track goes down into the valley, but keep straight ahead towards the lakes that will come

A view of the Eastnor Obelisk

into view as the path begins to descend into the main valley of Eastnor Park, which is used for camping and caravanning in the summer. Sheep are likely to be grazing here, and there are red deer which may also be seen.

Pass to the right side of the lakes, cross the small stream and go uphill along the driveway – with a speed limit of 15, which is unlikely to be relevant to walkers!

The drive leads steeply up to the Park Lodge house at the edge of the woodland. Turn right into the woods, over a cattle grid, and along a track which is to the left of the lodge house. The stony surfaced driveway is along The Ridgeway, an ancient track and possibly the line of an old salt route. Views from the top of this ridge of Wenlock limestone are restricted in summer by the trees on both sides, but in winter the landscape is more open. The woodland contains many yews, more commonly met in churchyards. The straight track climbs slightly and then levels off. Pass a point where paths come in from both left and right, and a yellow arrow appears, to indicate a Herefordshire County Council public footpath.

Shortly beyond this the drive divides, and the right fork goes down to Netherton Farm, but we keep straight ahead. Begin to climb again, and there may be noise of traffic away to the left, through the trees, along the A449. The track is still on the ridge top as it bends further round to the right, and the wood becomes narrower on both sides. Views down to Ockeridge Farm in the valley to the left can be seen through the trees. Swinyard Hill is over to the right, and then suddenly, straight ahead, the Herefordshire Beacon comes into sight through the trees.

Continue climbing and where the track splits, take the left fork and bend round to the left. The track bends left, and is soon joined by another track coming in from the right. Just keep going, as far as a house, a garden, and the main road. A public footpath goes straight across this road, the A449, but we turn right to walk along the verge for about 200m. When Beacon Lodge is on the right, turn left to pass Allfields. Follow the drive as it passes to the left of the house, and as the drive bends right, branch left on to a footpath into the woods. Descend along a clear path, to reach a stile and go out of the woods. Keep straight ahead along the left side of the field, and just before the end of the field turn right, where signed to British Camp car park. The path leads up through the woods to the toilet block and the Malvern Hills Hotel.

HOLLYBUSH PASS (159m or 524 ft) is on the A438 Tewkesbury to Ledbury road. Accessibility to Hollybush by public transport is very limited, with a less than daily bus service except for the Hills Hopper on summer weekends. There is plenty of car parking space at Hollybush and at Golden Valley, or on Hollybed and Castlemorton Commons.

Hollybush takes its name from the numerous holly bushes which grew in this area, and the bark of these trees was used as cattle fodder. The gap was a natural low area in the Malvern ridge, but was scraped and deepened by ice moving across the hills during a glacial phase of the Ice Age.

12

Midsummer Hill and the Commons

A walk round Golden Valley, Hollybed Common, Castlemorton Common, the Gullet and Midsummer Hill.

Distance: Just under 4 miles (6.5 km).
Maps: Landranger 150; Explorer 190.
Car Parking: See above.
Public Transport: None suitable.
Start/Finish: Hollybush Pass (GR 758368).
Refreshments: Nothing available, though you may meet an ice cream van on busy days in summer.

LEAVING the car park at the brow of Hollybush Pass cross over the road and turn left, to walk downhill, passing a delightful thatched cottage on the right hand side. Also on the right is an old mile stone, then the Hollybush Pottery, just before entering Worcestershire. Pass the cross roads with narrow roads leading off to the right and left, and the corrugated iron shed dated 1915 which is the Hollybush Church Room.

As the common opens up on the left, cross over and walk on the left fork of the common. Along the right fork is the Hollybush church if you wish to make a detour, and it is well worth a visit. Surrounded by a ha-ha and a stone wall, All Saints Church dates from 1860s, and was built for the workers who worked in Hollybush Quarry. It is built mainly of local stone, with some Bath stone.

Walk between Bank Cottage, a large modernised stone house on the left, and the tiny house on the right, at the top of the valley. This is Golden Valley

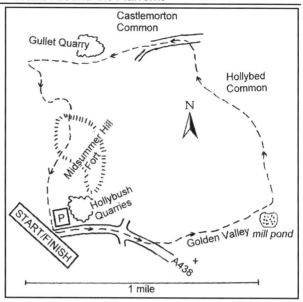

and contains a few other houses and barns down in the hollow to our right. A choice of routes is available here. Either stay on the left of the grassy slope to walk down to the left side of the Mill Pond — and then turn left alongside the hedge. Or stay on the right side and descend through bracken and trees to reach an old orchard. Go on beyond the pond and turn left along the embankment and cross the old sluice gate. Once beyond the pond, go left to the Information Board, and from here turn right.

The Mill Pond is home to an assortment of birds, moorhens, ducks and geese — and is popular with picnickers and fishermen. Grinding corn continued until 1943, though the mill has since been demolished. The pond was cleaned out by the Conservators in 1972 and 1975, and was enlarged and restructured. Walk away from the pond to come alongside the hedge, with a cultivated field just over the fence, and the common extending away to our right. Keep close to the edge of this common, Hollybed Common, and after a slight climb, turn left to pass between two houses. Follow the stony driveway of these houses for about 30 yards, and where it bends right, keep straight ahead staying close to the hedge. Gradually climb up to the narrow road on Castlemorton Common.

Turn left and walk alongside the road, with Swinyard Hill straight ahead. There may be an ice cream van here on summer weekends, and hang gliders floating around from the hill top.

Where the road splits, take the right fork, and the narrow tarmac-surfaced track will lead past a cottage to the Gullet quarry, which ceased production in 1977. It is of great interest to geologists, with Pre-Cambrian Malvernian rocks and also Silurian rocks on top. The old Pre Cambrians include red granite, grey and white granite, as well as dolerite. Since closing down the quarry site has been cleared by the Conservators and is a popular playground area especially on a hot summer's day, though it has proved dangerous to swim in the very cold water which has a maximum depth of over 100 feet. *Do not swim* *here, however tempting it may seem.*Pass to the left of the lake and out on to the broad stony track leading up through Gullet Wood. This is rich in daffodils and bluebells in the spring.

At the top of the Gullet (204m or 671 ft), just before the gate which marks the boundary of Eastnor Park, is a major cross paths. Turn left and continue to climb steadily along the stony track.The Obelisk can soon be seen to the right and as views open up to the left, Gullet Quarry and Swinyard Hill can be seen. Just past the house down in the hollow on the left hand side, and ignoring the steep path straight ahead, turn left off the track and follow the path alongside the hedge and fence. This leads up to the top of the hill.

Pass the National Trust sign situated on the outermost mound and ditch of Midsummer Hill encampment which probably dates from about 300BC and contained over 200 hut sites. The iron age fort is quite well documented as a result of a dig from 1965-70, though much more could still be discovered if further digging were permitted. The main rampart and ditch on Midsummer Hill have two ancient entrances, at the north and south gates. The Iron Age age settlement also enclosed the neighbouring peak of Hollybush Hill which is out of sight beyond the trees on the east side of our route. A total of 22 acres was enclosed within the earthworks.

The path soon splits but do not fork left along the path which goes

The Gullet

downhill, unless you wish to investigate the old pillow mound and the main part of the hill fort on Hollybush Hill. Keep straight ahead and up on to the hill top, with good views of the Obelisk and Eastnor Castle to the right, and across the plain to Bredon and the Cotswolds to the left. Also admire the view back northwards along the Malvern Ridge.

The small shelter on the summit (284m or 932 ft) contains a plaque saying that the Iron Age hill fort was given to the National Trust in 1923 in memory of Captain Reginald Somers Cocks M.C., from Eastnor.

Go straight on, across the edge of the hill fort and follow the narrow stony path leading downhill, between bracken and shrubby trees, descending gently at first but then the path levels slightly before bending to the right (a few yards to the left of the path is the huge hollow of Hollybush Quarry which closed in 1977 and is now partially flooded. This was quarried for road gravel, and contained pre-Cambrian rocks at the bottom, but with younger Silurian rocks higher up). The path leads down to the road through large trees and then a grassy slope, and can be quite slippery if wet.

A good view of the thatched cottage passed at the beginning of the walk will be seen during this descent back to the starting point, as well as a clear view of Raggedstone Hill. If you are still feeling energetic you could go straight on to follow Walk 13 up to the top of that hill too.

The Commons of Castlemorton and Hollybed are managed by the Malvern Hills Conservators, and these commons considerably extend the limits of their land. Castlemorton Common was bought in 1962 and 1966, and part of it is designated an S.S.S.I. The area of scrub and grassland is being maintained as a common, which requires sheep to graze it and human involvement to remove scrub and tree growth. In spite of its name, common land is not available for anyone or everyone to use. It is a relic of the time when the Lord of the Manor controlled the land, and his tenants and freeholders would have had some rights to use the common. In 1884, an Act of Parliament made the common land available to the Public, but only for access, and not for grazing or any other activities.

Hollybush Common

13

The Most Southerly Hills

This walk visits the two most southerly hills of the Malvern Range, Raggedstone and Chase End, which are lower than those further north. They are like a promontory of high ground stretching southwards towards Gloucestershire.

> **Distance:** Only 3 miles (5 km), but does include two very steep climbs, and one very steep descent.
> **Maps:** Landranger 150; Explorer 190.
> **Car Parking:** See page 69.
> **Public Transport:** Nothing suitable.
> **Start/Finish:** GR 758368.
> **Refreshments:** Nothing available, though you may meet an ice cream van on busy days in summer.

FROM THE CAR PARK, walk back to the road and turn right for about 150 yards. Pass the bus shelter on the left and at the gate just beyond it turn left into the woods. The track immediately splits – take the right fork – and start to climb. After about 50 yards, at the cross path which comes in from the left, turn right for about 10 yards and then go off this clear path, and climb steeply to the left, up a grassy patch.

After just a few yards, bend left along a narrow grassy path between trees (ash, hawthorn, rowan) and shrubs. Continue to climb up to a grassy and mossy area, through the bracken, to emerge on the more open slopes which lead up to the summit of Raggedstone, at a height of 254m (833 ft). Views to the left look into Hollybush Quarry and up to the summit of Midsummer Hill beyond. The Obelisk can be clearly seen and there are magnificent views over Herefordshire.

The rocky summit is part of a ridge and the onward route is to the right, heading southwards towards Chase End Hill with its triangulation point.

Before moving on, note that just over to the east is the second of the rocky summit peaks which helped to give Raggedstone Hill its name. The second peak is separated by a valley from the one on which we are standing.

Be sure to stay in the sun if it is shining, in order to avoid the curse of Raggedstone! The legend of the hill is clearly told in *The Shadow of the Ragged Stone*, a novel by Charles F. Grindrod, which was published in 1888. A monk from Little Malvern had fallen in love with a local girl, and broken his vows of chastity. As a penance his Prior told him to crawl on his hands and knees up to the summit of Raggedstone each day. Eventually, and not surprisingly, just before he died he had become fed up with his punishment. One day, instead of praying when he reached the top, he placed a curse on the hill. 'May all upon whom the shadow of this stone falls untimely die.' It is claimed that the shadow of the hill had fallen on the Member of Parliament William Huskisson before he was accidentally killed by George Stephenson's steam train *The Rocket*.

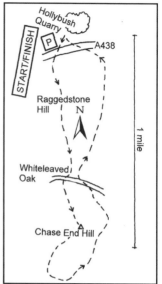

So walk on quickly, following the summit ridge in a southerly direction. Just to the left is a good remnant of the Red Earl's Dyke, cut out of the solid rock. As you follow the narrow stony path there are further remnants of this remarkable embankment. The descent is steep

View over Whiteleaved Oak towards Raggedstone Hill

and may be slippery on the loose stony surface. The path is through gorse and soon drops down to tree level, where the path is less stony and tree roots seem to be holding the path together more successsfully so there is less erosion.

At the bottom of the steep descent join a broad track, which we will be using for the return journey to Hollybush. Turn right along this track, pass a house ('Never mind the dog, beware of the owner'), go through a gate with an M.H.C. notice on it, pass another house and emerge on to the road in the delightful and secluded hamlet of Whiteleaved Oak, where Herefordshire, Worcestershire and Gloucestershire all meet. It is believed that an oak tree with variegated leaves looked whitish and gave its name to this hamlet. Some of the houses are half timbered and date from seventeenth or eighteenth century.

Turn right and walk along the road which soon bends to the left. Just past the letter box, turn left along the path with the Gloucestershire County Council notice saying 'No Horses. Public Footpath Only'.

This leads alongside the lovely house and garden of Cider Mill Cottage, and on to a narrow path (which can be very muddy in winter) between hedges and small trees which meet overhead to make a tunnel in summer. Next is an area of bracken and scattered trees, and a short but steep ascent up a grassy slope to the triangulation point, 191m (626 ft). Chase End Hill has sometimes been referred to as the Gloucestershire Beacon. Pause to admire the views of Whiteleaved Oak down in the hollow and the twin peaks of Raggedstone Hill beyond. You walked over the left of the two peaks.

The name Chase End indicates it was the hill at the end of the Chase, and in this case it was the southern limit. The Chase was an area of hunting allocated to someone by the King. It was William the Conqueror who had established the Malvern Chase area as a Royal Forest. The whole of Malvern Chase must have been forested at first, but some areas were cleared as enclosures for domestic animals. These enclosures resembled the parkland to be seen on many large estates. Deer would be allowed into the enclosures for food, but then they could escape back to the forest via deer leaps. Gradually over the centuries, woodland was removed and some of the Chase was turned into common land, by Charles I and others.

From the summit the path swings half right (south-west) and continues gently down the grassy slope. Views ahead to the Forest of Dean and the clump of trees on May Hill are likely to be visible. Where the grassy path begins to level off and broaden out, turn left and walk into the woods.

Descend a few yards into the woods to a cross paths. A large gate is to the right and just beyond is a small gate leading straight downhill. However, we turn left along a broad track through the trees, with many sweet chestnut, some sycamore and oak. After about 200 yards reach a gate and soon another gate across the track. Continue straight ahead through these woods, which contain some very tall sweet chestnut, ash and beech, and many smaller trees too. A path comes in from the right but continue along the main track, and it will soon begin to bend round to the left before descending to the road by two small cottages, one of which is built of local stone and recently modernised.

At the road turn left, and walk uphill for 300-400 yards into Whiteleaved Oak, to reach the point where you joined this road on the outward journey. Turn right here along the stony track and through the gate, but do not fork left up the narrow path you used earlier. Just keep going along the broad horizontal track and into the woods.

Pass an old quarry on the left, and descend slightly by the open patch on the left, before beginning to climb. Following the obvious track keep climbing steadily until the track levels off to pass along the side of Raggedstone Hill, with a steep slope up to the left of the path, and steeply down to the right. There are many magnificent trees on these slopes, and these trees provide welcome cooling shade on a hot summer day, or warming shelter on a cold mid winter walk. This wood is called Ladywell Coppice and contains a plantation of Lodgepole pine and Norway spruce in addition to the usual deciduous trees. Evidence of former coppicing can be seen here as well as in the woods alongside Chase End Hill passed earlier.

Continue on this well-marked path which, shortly after a cottage standing high on your left, swings to the left and begins its descent, passing the Old Post Office and postbox just before reaching the road, directly opposite the main entrance to the Hollybush Quarry. If you are intending to complete Walk 12 as well, turn right here, but otherwise turn left and walk up the hill to the top of Hollybush Pass and the car park you started from. On the way you will pass Hollybush Pottery, and an old milestone nearly in the hedge at the side of the pavement, before reaching the signpost for Herefordshire.

Three walks from Ledbury

LEDEBERGE was mentioned in the Domesday Book and has been a flourishing market town, set in the heart of beautiful countryside, since about 1120. Ledbury is noted for its fine collection of black and white buildings, and as the birthplace of John Masefield. Early British settlers built camps on hills nearby, and the town was involved in fighting during the Civil War. In April 1645, Prince Rupert and his men surprised the Roundheads and fierce fighting took place in and around Ledbury. The town is well linked by road to Worcester, Hereford and Gloucester, and has regular train services to London and to Birmingham.

14

A Ledbury Town Walk

This walk includes many of the historical features of Ledbury as well as a nearby hillside, with views of the town and across to the Malvern Hills.

Distance: Nearly 3 miles (4.5 km), but will be quite slow because of numerous interesting features on the route.
Maps: Landranger 150; Explorer 190.
Car Parking: Ledbury central car park (GR710376).
Public Transport: Trains and buses to Ledbury. If arriving by train, after leaving the station approach turn left into Ledbury. As you walk towards the town (about half a mile) look out for the fine cruck framed house (No. 235). This ancient, and rather primitive form of house construction, used a pair of arched tree trunks, joined at the top to provide a frame for the building. Entering the centre of the town look out also for the late sixteenth century (though recently rebuilt after a fire) Seven Stars Inn. Cross the road to reach the prominent clock tower on the right.
Start/Finish: Ledbury central car park (GR710376).
Refreshments: Pubs and cafés in Ledbury.

FROM the main car park go on to Bye Street and turn right, towards the clock tower.

Start from here if you have arrived by train.

This is the Barrett Browning Institute and contains the Library. Turn right at the main cross roads and pass St. Katharine's Hospital which was founded in 1232 by Bishop Hugh Foliot, to house the poor and look after the sick. None of the original alms-houses survive, but the present ones date from the mid-nineteenth century, built to the design of Robert Smirke, the architect of Eastnor Castle. Part of the hospital still remains from the fourteenth century. Wordsworth wrote a sonnet about St. Katharine, who was Katharine Audley, Patron Saint of Ledbury.

Just in front of St.Katharine's is an old drinking trough for horses, with a lower level for dogs. Continue along this side of the road to the Feathers Inn which dates from 1560, when it was two houses. It became an important stopping place on the Cheltenham to Aberystwyth stagecoach route.

Cross over the road and walk back on the other side, to visit the Market House, the most prominent building on High Street. It was built in the 1640s, standing on sixteen chestnut pillars cut down from the Malvern forest. The open ground floor was used as a market, and also as an information centre, where notices could be pinned. The upstairs was the Town Hall for many years and was used as a small theatre and for public meetings. There was originally a third storey beneath the roof, used for storing corn.

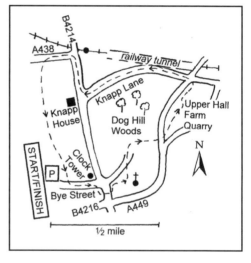

From the Market House turn right into Church Lane. The first building on the left dates from around 1500 and houses the Council offices. This is open to visitors (11 am to 1 pm and 2 to 4 pm, Mondays to Fridays and Sundays 2 to 5 pm) and admission is free, to see the Painted Room. The paintings were unknown until 1988 when refurbishment work on the building revealed a room full of wall paintings. The paintings have religious themes, and probably date from the sixteenth century. The room and house were lived in by the constable, and the Painted Room may have been used as the Court Room, though much of the history of the room in recent centuries is not fully known.

The historic cobbled Church Lane, popular with television companies and photographers, contains many other fine buildings. The Prince of Wales public house dates from the fifteenth or sixteenth century: the Old Grammar School is now a Heritage Centre, with an exhibition room upstairs. On the right is the Butcher Row Folk Museum.

Windows in Ledbury Parish Church

The church is at the end of the lane and contains many interesting features. For instance the 76 ft tower is detached from the church. It dates from the thirteenth century, and the 126 ft spire on top of it was built between 1727 and 1734. It contains a fine carillon which plays at three-hourly intervals (9 am, 12 noon, 3 pm, 6 pm). Parts of the church are Norman, and the original church was probably built on the site of an earlier Saxon church. The west door has fine carvings and there are many interesting features inside, but outstanding for most people are the superb collection of windows.

Go back to leave the churchyard and turn right to walk through the small walled gardens. Just inside the gate is a solid oak post commemorating the fifty oak trees which were planted in Ledbury in 2002 to celebrate the Golden Jubilee. Go out of the gate at the far side, and turn left to go uphill, with Upper Hall Close on the left. When the road bends left, keep straight ahead along a surfaced track into Dog Hill Woods, with a small plaque on the right wall to tell you that this is Green Lane, and was the pack horse route to Worcester. Dog

Hill Woods is noted for its spring flowers, especially snowdrops, bluebells and wood anemones.

Almost at the top of the climb is a cross paths, where a right turn by a seat will lead along a broad sunken track with many tree roots showing. After about 100 yards go right over a stile and follow the fence downhill through a grassy field, with views of Herefordshire Beacon and woods ahead. At the bottom go through an old iron gate, pass to the right of a small pond and cross over the minor road to Coddington and on to a narrow footpath.

This leads into the woods which are rich in bird and flower life. Ascend along a fairly straight stretch through the woods, and then descend slightly to a cross tracks and turn left. Pass a quarry entrance on the right, though detour here if you wish to look at the outcrop of very clear layers of rock in Upper Hall Farm Quarry. The rocks are Upper Wenlock limestone and some shale beds, and the quarry is an S.S.S.I. because of its interesting geology.

Continue on the track beyond the quarry for about 50 yards and on the right is a surprising flight of concrete steps, with a handrail, and a wealth of wild flowers all around. Go up the steps, and follow the clear path through to a gate. Then walk along the field margin to a stile and out on to the road at a crossroads.

Turn left, not sharp left on the Hereford road which runs almost parallel to our path through the field, but along the road with no signpost, to the right of a house. Soon come to a narrow road sign (*beware of traffic along here as at the time of writing it is being used as a short cut rat-run*), and just keep going up a slight hill to be joined by a road from the right. We are now leaving Cut Throat Lane, and on the left is the end of Green Lane, the broad track through Dog Hill Woods which we walked along for a short distance earlier.

To get off the road, go past the gate and into the woods for about 20 yards and then turn right. Follow the narrow path which is parallel and quite close to the road, and stay on this until reaching a small flight of steps near the 30 sign. Go on to the road (unavoidable here) and turn left, to descend along Knapp Lane. At the main street, the large black and white house opposite is Knapp House, birthplace of John Masefield.

Turn right here to walk towards the station, and just before the station turn left along the path between the railway line and the road. We are now on the Ledbury Town Trail which follows the route of the Ledbury to Gloucester railway which closed in 1962. The path leads up slightly and then bends left to get on to the old embankment. From the embankment we look down on modern housing developments to the right, and occasional views open up through the trees. As we approach the centre of the town, cross the footbridge above a main road, and then on the left is a playground area and a small skate park, and good views of the church spire. Walk on as far as Bye Street and turn left passing the Fire Station to return to your starting point.

15

To Eastnor

A walk through farmland and woods to the village of Eastnor with an opportunity to visit the Castle with its attractive grounds. (See the box below for opening times.)

Distance: Nearly 5 miles (8 km), plus any distance walked in Eastnor Park.
Maps: Landranger 149/150; Explorer 190.
Car Parking: See Walk 14.
Public Transport: See Walk 14.
Start/Finish: Market House, Ledbury (GR711377).
Refreshments: See Walk 14.
Special Feature: Eastnor Castle and grounds. Open on Sundays from Easter to the end of September; Bank Holiday Mondays; Sunday to Friday during July and August, from 11 a.m. till 5 p.m.

FROM THE MARKET HOUSE walk down Church Lane. Pass along the left side of the church, between the church and the separate spire, and turn right behind the church to reach the pathway between stone walls. This leads out to the main road, and a plaque on the wall tells you that this pathway is Cabbage Lane, sometimes known as Capuchin Lane.

Turn left along the road, past the Police Station, and after about 100 yards cross over and go right at the footpath sign, up a few steps and along a narrow track into Coneygree Wood, between two

Ledbury Market House

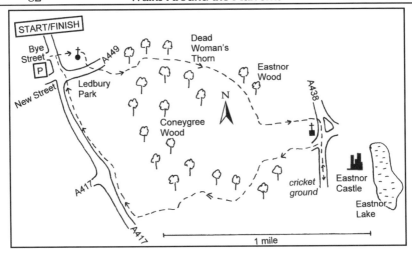

driveways to houses. It is very muddy for a few yards, because of a spring. It becomes a narrow and sunken pathway, overhung by trees. Climb slightly and pass through a gateway, and when the path splits, take the left fork which is more or less straight ahead.

The path is on the right side just above a deep sunken trackway, and climbs up to a cross track. Go straight across this and along the path climbing up through the trees, with the sunken track still to the left for a few more yards, before it bends further away.

Keep going up for a steady climb as far as a horizontal broad stony track. Turn left along this and after about 30 yards turn right on a stony path which climbs slightly. Go right through a small wooden gate and immediately left to continue more or less straight ahead, with a hedge and trees on the left and an open area to the right.

Follow the field margin as the path bends round to the right at the first corner of the field, and then at the next corner leave the field by turning down left for a few yards along a track leading into a small patch of trees. Go through an old gate and straight on at the cross paths. The track heads downhill and bends to the right, and then out into an open field, with woods straight ahead. Walk down the hill, along the left side of this open grassy patch, passing an old brick barn with a corrugated iron roof on the left – referred to as Dead Woman's Thorn on the Explorer map. Just beyond this, views open out to the Herefordshire Beacon and the Malvern ridge stretching northwards. At the end of the grassy field go over a wooden stile, pass through a few trees and climb slightly. A track comes in from the right but keep straight ahead to the top of the hill, and then descend slightly and bend to the left. Go through the metal gate at the bottom and straight across the middle of an open field, with the woods of Eastnor Hill to the left, and a small house up to the right.

At the end of the field go through a gate and along a short track, then turn left into an open field, with wonderful views to Eastnor Castle, Eastnor Church, the Obelisk and the line of the Malvern Hills. Follow the track downhill aiming to the left of the church. As the track bends right keep straight ahead along the field margin, with a hedge to the right. Once beyond the houses and the church, turn right down a few steps and out of the field to walk along the narrow road to the church gate. On the left before reaching the church gate is an impressive avenue of lime trees.

Visit the red sandstone church of St. John the Baptist, which was rebuilt in 1852, though the tower dates from the fourteenth century and the south doorway is Norman, with trumpet scallop capitals. The clock and chimes are a memorial to those who died in World War I, and the screen is a memorial to Captain Reginald Somers-Cocks M.C. who also died in the war. Another plaque is a memorial to Louisa Humphries B.E.M. (1877-1970), the village postmistress for 63 years.

From the church walk along the road, passing the school (built by Robert Smirke) on the left, and turn right along the minor road by the small green. A few yards along here is a surfaced driveway to Eastnor Pottery and the Eastnor Estate Office which is our route for the return to Ledbury, but before going there fork left along the road which leads round to the entrance to Eastnor Castle. The village cricket pitch is on the right, opposite the entrance to the Garden Centre and the Castle.

The castle overlooks the lake and deer park, and was designed for the 1st Earl Somers by Sir Robert Smirke, who was also responsible for the design of the British Museum. It contains a fine collection of armour, paintings and tapestries, and has a Children's Adventure Playground.

After visiting the castle, retrace your steps nearly 200 yards, and with the church directly ahead across a field, turn left along the driveway which has a bridleway finger post. (EA 1) The route passes the Eastnor Estate Office, the barns and the Eastnor Pottery, which is in one of the old farm buildings. The old farm is a magnificent building, with tall square brick chimneys. Walk past the farm buildings and along the now stony driveway. The track bends slightly left and goes uphill a little – and provides stunning views across to the right – the route we were walking on our way down to the church. Pass a grove of tall poplars on the right, and ignore the track going off to the right to a metal gate. Follow the main track for nearly 200 yards before going right through a small gate into the long but fairly narrow field. Head diagonally left up to the far top corner of the field, just to the right of the buildings.

Go through a metal gate and straight on past the buildings, and just before reaching another metal gate, bend round to the right following the bridleway, with trees on the right and an open field to the left. This leads round to a gate, and the path ahead is diagonally down to the right towards the bottom corner of the field. Walking down through this field, there are woods to the right, straight ahead and to the left. As you approach the bottom corner you will see the small gate to enable us to leave the field.

Go through the gate, across a plank footbridge and through another gate into the woods. The path winds through this mixed woodland, mainly deciduous but with a few conifers, and soon joins a broad track. Just keep going (left) along here and at the Coneygree Wood sign, where four routes meet, keep straight ahead. Pass through a gateway and go downhill to join a stony track which is the driveway to a house up to the right. We just go straight ahead along this track, passing a house on the left and orchard on the right, before reaching the main road, A417.

Turn right and walk back into Ledbury. A broad grass verge between the road and the footpath will separate you from the traffic for most of the way. Pass the John Masefield High School on the left, and before reaching the traffic lights, on the right hand side is the magnificent black and white Elizabethan house called Ledbury Park. The plaque on the wall says it is was Prince Rupert's Headquarters during the Battle of Ledbury in 1645 during the Civil War. Built by Edward Skinner about 1595 it became the home of the Biddulph family 1688-1941.

Opposite Ledbury Park, at the end of New Street (so named about AD1232) is an early seventeenth century timber framed building with the first floor supported on posts over the pavement. Continue along High Street to pass The Feathers Hotel, dated at 1560, before reaching the starting point of the walk.

16

A Poets' Walk

A walk to Wellington Heath, passing the homes of John Masefield and Elizabeth Barrett Browning. Both of these poets enjoyed the rural surroundings of the Ledbury area, grew up with a love of the countryside, and were influenced and inspired in some of their writing by their own experiences nearby.

Distance: 6 miles (10 km).
Maps: Landranger 149; Explorer 190.
Car Parking: See Walk 14.
Public Transport: Trains and buses to Ledbury.
If commencing from the railway station start reading from ★ on page 86.
Start/Finish: Ledbury town centre (GR711377).
Refreshments: Farmers Arms, Wellington Heath; pubs and cafés in Ledbury.

WALK out of Ledbury centre heading northwards along The Homend, towards the railway station. Along this road there is a fine collection of old buildings, and narrow alleyways leading off the main road.

Before reaching the station, opposite the end of Knapp Lane, is Knapp House, the birthplace on 1st June 1878 of John Masefield, who was the Poet Laureate from 1930-1967. Although he went to sea at the age of 13, and subsequently worked in New York when he was 17, he never forgot his early years.

He later became a journalist and then began to experiment with his writing. It was in 1911 that he produced *The Everlasting Mercy*, his first great narrative poem. Much of his writing was about the countryside and especially the Malvern Hills, which are so clearly to be seen from near his birthplace.

In his poem *On Malvern Hill*, he wrote:

> The leaves whirl in the wind's riot
> Beneath the Beacon's jutting spur

Masefield's love of the countryside is shown in many of his poems, for instance in *The Hill*:

> I see yon harebells, foxgloves, brooks,
> All glistening from the rain,
> The cruising kestrels and the rooks
> And haunted hill again.

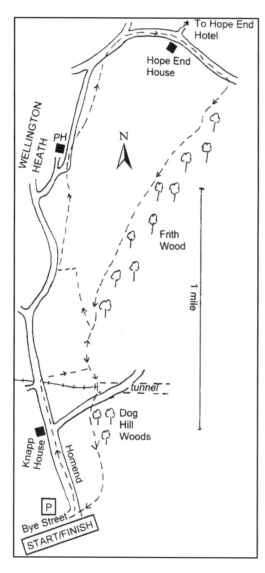

★ *Start here if arriving by train. From the station approach turn right to go under the railway bridge.*

Just past the railway bridge go right over a stile, and walk along the right margin of the field. Continue straight ahead over two more stiles and walk up to the margin of the woods. Turn left here (*LR21* and *LR18*) and walk along the top edge of the fields, with good views to the left and the wood on the right.

At the end of this field, go over a stile and walk through the garden (yes, through the garden) of Little Frith Cottage. Leave it via a small kissing gate, and emerge into an orchard. Go straight into the orchard and head towards a brick house at the far end. This large orchard is one of few remaining in the area, whereas in the past orchards and hop fields (*known in Herefordshire as hopyards*) were numerous, Herefordshire being second only to Kent for fruit and hop production. Apples were a particularly popular fruit which sustained the large cider production in the county. Ahead and to the right a converted oast house can be seen, a relic of the hop producing days.

Just before the brick house turn left along the drive and walk towards the road. The footpath goes off to the right (*LR17*) just before the road, across a grassy field, used for camping and caravanning in the summer, and into another orchard. Keep to the left margin of this field for about 50 yards, then follow the main track as it heads right and then left through the orchard. Descend to a small stream and cross this at a small stiled footbridge, then turn right along the edge of the field. Pass over a stile and straight on across the next small field, through a tiny gate and diagonally up to the left aiming for the top of the line of conifers. This will lead to a stile by an iron gate, and out on to a driveway. After a few yards this reaches a road, then turn right and walk through part of Wellington Heath. There are a few attractive old houses as well as many smart newer ones.

At the Farmers Arms Inn and Restaurant the road bends right over a small stream and past a V.R. post box, then bends left towards the telephone box. Before the phone, turn right along a surfaced driveway for about ten yards before going left on to a steeply climbing grassy path, between hedges. This leads up past a house on the right and on to a stony drive. Walk along here, passing a few houses. Magnificent views open up to the right, across the valley towards Frith Wood.

At 'The Cottage' the main drive bends down to the left, but keep straight ahead to the end of the track, where there is a stile. Go over this, and along the left side of the field, admiring the views of Herefordshire Beacon to the right, and continue to two stiles and the road.

Turn right and walk along the road, passing an old pump and seat on the right, then forking right at the junction, following the sign to Hope End. The deep sheltered valley is down to the right. Pass the large complex of Hope End Farm on the right, and then the entrance to Hope End on the left, and just beyond along the road is a cutting with exposures of some fossiliferous rocks from the the Ludlovian series of the Silurian period.

Now a private house after a few years as a Country Hotel, Hope End was the home of Elizabeth Barrett Browning for nineteen years. Elizabeth was born in Northumberland but brought to live here when she was three. Her father, Edward Moulton Barrett bought the 475 acre estate in 1809 and almost immediately built a Moorish style palace with turrets and minarets, whilst the old house became the stables and coach house. Unfortunately his grand house has not survived, though the beautiful parkland still remains. Elizabeth was the eldest of twelve children and adored by her father. She was quite a tomboy until a fall from a pony at the age of fifteen injured her back, and seemed to permanently affect her health. Her gift for writing became apparent at an early age, with verses being written even when she was only six. She read widely and wrote steadily, and her father had some of her work published. Her mother died in 1828 and then father had serious financial problems so the family left Hope End and moved to Sidmouth in 1832. Undoubtedly her years at Ledbury affected much of her writing, and Elizabeth was always a great lover of the countryside.

> Hills, vales, woods settled in silver mist
> Farms, granges, doubled up amongst the hills
> And cottage chimneys smoking from the woods.

In old age, she thought it would be a mistake to return to live in this area, and wrote: 'It would be a mockery, like the taking back of a broken flower to its stalk'.

Walk along the road, through the cutting , and look out for views ahead of the Eastnor Obelisk. The road goes downhill, and on the right are two wooden gates and two footpaths. *CW57* goes across the field to the left, but our route is *CW56*, along the stony track between hedges. After nearly a quarter mile, where the main path starts to bend to the left into Frith Wood, fork right off the driveway on to a narrow path (*LR21*), which follows the edge of the woods, with delightful views over the large Hope valley to the right. The word Hope is derived from the Old English for a valley, often an enclosed or blind valley, such as this one.

The path continues between the edge of Frith Wood on the left and fields on the right, for half a mile to a complex of barns and buildings, and to a

Ledbury Viaduct

quarry on the side of the path. The rock here is also Ludlovian and contains many shells (brachipods) and other fossils.

The path leads on to a drive by a house and garden where recent modernisation work has been taking place, but keep straight ahead along the drive. Just before reaching the house with the oast towers, seen earlier on the outward journey, fork left off the drive on a grassy path leading through to a field margin. Continue along this margin, still with the woods to the left, and now the orchards are to the right. There are excellent views of the railway viaduct over to the right, built from 1859-1861, to carry the railway line to Hereford.

We are now about 200 yards higher up the orchard than we were on the outward journey and at the end of this field, retrace steps through the garden crossed earlier, via a small kissing gate and over a stile. Walk along the field margin, but do not turn right at the end of the field to retrace the route we used earlier. Go straight ahead, over a stile and on to a driveway. Frith Wood House is up to the left, but turn right and walk along the drive, over the railway line which has just entered the Ledbury tunnel, and through to the road.

Cross straight over the road and up a few steps to follow the path straight ahead through the woods. A fairly horizontal path leads us through Dog Hill Woods, with roof tops to the right. Reach a major cross paths, mentioned in Walk 14, and keep straight ahead and descend into the town, close to the church and Church Lane.

Four Walks from Upton upon Severn

SEEN FROM AFAR the tower of the old church and the spire of the new make Upton very distinctive and prominent. The town grew because of the river traffic, and took its name as the *ton* (settlement) up stream from Ripple. The first written record of the town is in 897, and the Domesday Book included Upton as part of the Ecclesiastical Manor of Ripple.

Growth of the town was not only because of the river route, but also because of the crossing point, by ford and by ferry, until the first bridge was built. The earliest recorded bridge seems to have been a wooden structure in the fifteenth century. The importance of the crossing point was emphasised in the Civil War, as a major battle was fought here, on 29th August 1651. The Royalist guards were taken by surprise, and Cromwell captured the bridge, just before marching on to Worcester to the final battle of the war.

The town is a mixture of old medieval, Tudor, Georgian and Jacobean, with many modern developments thrown in. River trade was very important in the past, and is important again today for the tourist industry. Riverside pubs were popular with the boatmen plying their trade up and down the Severn in the eighteenth century, and they are still popular with modern day boatmen and women.

The river dominates life in Upton for much of the year, and every winter there is the threat of floods to contend with. The riverside meadows are flooded annually, but many of the houses also have to be prepared with sandbags, but these prove indadequate defence against the rising water in some years.

The central part of the town nowadays, in addition to the bridge, is the old church tower, known as the Pepperpot. This is the thirteenth century tower of the ancient parish church, which was given to the Malvern Hills District Council by the Diocese of Worcester in 1980, on condition it was repaired and maintained in good condition. The church tower formerly had a spire, but this was replaced by Anthony Keck's cupola in 1770. When the nave of this church was dismantled in 1937 the churchyard was laid out as a garden. In the garden and adjacent to the tower is the Heritage Centre. The garden also contains a statue of Admiral Sir William Tennant, one of Upton's most famous and illustrious inhabitants. He was the senior naval officer at Dunkirk, at the beginning of World War II.

The four walks from Upton all begin at the main car park near the bridge and the Pepperpot, and they are circuits of 3, 4, 5 and 7 miles in length. Any two could be joined together as a figure of eight or double loop to enable you to find a longer walk if desired. It would be possible to complete one walk in a morning and return to Upton for lunch in one of the many pubs, then have a second walk in the afternoon.

17

Hanley Castle

This walk can be comfortably completed in two hours, with a visit to Hanley Castle church.

Distance: Just over 3 miles (5 km).
Maps: Landranger 150; Explorer 190.
Car Parking: The main car park near the bridge and the Pepperpot.
Public Transport: Bus service 363/364 from Worcester; 372 service from Worcester, Sundays and Bank Holidays.
Start/Finish: Car park near the bridge at GR850407.
Refreshments: Pubs, cafés and restaurants in Upton.

L EAVE the Upton upon Severn car park and turn left along the main road to walk away from Upton. Pass the garage and walk over the small stream Pool Brook, near its confluence with the River Severn. Just beyond Pool House Caravan Park turn right on the footpath which leads through a gate and alongside the allotments. After about 100 yards the path bends left, with the river just to the right. Go over a stile and turn right to walk along the right side of the field – straight on really.

A footpath diversion has taken the path nearer to the river than formerly, and leads in about a quarter of a mile to a stile, and across a lawn, with a large oak tree to the left of the path. Reach the driveway which is the end of Quay Lane, a former crossing point of the river. Turn left here and walk up Quay Lane, passing a few houses, and then the large farm, Herbert's Farm on the left, which has been restored

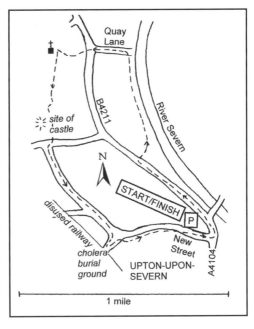

and partially rebuilt. Notice the three tall chimneys.

At the main road there is an old weathered cross of uncertain origin on the right of Quay Lane. Go straight across the road here and along Bowling Green Lane. The playing fields and school are on the right, and at the end of the road, take the path into the churchyard, through the kissing gate.

St. Mary's Church stands alongside the old village centre with a small green. There has probably been a church on this site since the tenth century and parts of the present nave date from the fourteenth century. The High Altar was dedicated to the Bishop of Worcester in 1280. The squat tower is built of bricks and some sandstone, and the eastern part of the nave is also brick, but the west is of a different stone. Inside are some striking and distinctive stained glass windows. Alongside the churchyard is part of the ancient village school, as well as some early seventeenth century timber framed almshouses.

Hanley Castle Grammar School was founded in 1523 or earlier, and a plaque on the school claims a foundation as early as 1326. The oldest surviving building dates from the early seventeenth century. The Victorian part is from 1868 and there have been modern additions. Recent changes to the school include the ending of boarding, the admission of girls, and the abolition of the eleven plus examination in 1974, meant the school changed from a grammar school to Hanley Castle High School.

Hanley Castle

Walk on alongside the path which passes close to the eastern end of the church, and leads through a kissing gate (not the one used when arriving at the church but at the same end of the graveyard). Follow the hedge on the right and bend right then left but still following the edge of the field and heading southwards. After about 300 yards leave the field through an old iron kissing gate, and go right over a stile at the side of an iron gate. Cross over the stream, Pool Brook, and straight on over another stile by an iron gate.

After a further 20 yards, before reaching the two stone gate posts, turn left over the stile and walk along the embankment. The stream is to the left, and a dry moat to the right with the site of the castle beyond, though with no visible remains. The castle was built by King John probably for use as a hunting lodge in the Malvern Chase, and he stayed in this castle for a time in 1209 and 1213. Stones from this castle were used in building the 1605 bridge in Upton.

Go over the next stile, by an iron gate, and straight on down the drive of Birley Mill, and at the road turn right. After 20 yards turn left on New Street Lane which leads back to Upton. Pass Little Mill Cottage, and join a wider road, but keep straight ahead. The course of the winding stream on your left is attractively marked out with willows. The road splits and between the two roads is a stile which leads to your path back to Upton.

Before crossing this stile, detour right for about 40 yards to the line of the old railway, which can be located by its embankment. This was the branch line from Malvern to Tewkesbury, opened in 1864. Beyond the railway the footpath passes alongside a Severn-Trent Water installation, and 20-30 yards further along the track, over the hedge on the right, is the Cholera Burial Ground, from the Upton plague of 1832. This is surrounded by a small low brick wall: a plaque on the wall merely states 'Cholera burial ground 1832'.

Return to the stile, cross and continue towards Upton, on the path which follows the old causeway, with the road just a few yards to the left, at a lower level. The path reaches two stiles and then continues along the left margin of a field to another stile and the edge of the built up area. This is New Street and on the left is number 36, the Goom Stool Cottage, where the Ducking Stool was located in former times. On the building nearly opposite number 36 is a plaque on the wall – 'This is the site of the Goom Stool Cottages which were built at the end of the fifteenth century and demolished in 1882. Near here was a dirty pool where the ancient cucking or ducking stool stood in which slander-ous women were tied and ducked up and down in the water'.

At the end of New Street turn left along High Street. Across the road is the Talbot Head Hotel and then The White Lion Hotel, which features in the 1749 novel *Tom Jones* by Henry Fielding, thought by many to be one of the all time great novels. It is believed that the White Lion is the inn referred to in this story.

Turn left along Church Road to walk back to the car park and the starting point, passing the Tourist Information Centre, then Cromwell's chocolate shop on the left and a plaque on the wall marking the event that on 29th August 1651 Oliver Cromwell was greeted here 'With abundance of joy and extraordinary shouting – after the decisive battle of Upton'. Cromwell's is a sixteenth century building, one of the oldest in Upton.

Next door to it is the Tudor House Museum of Upton Past and Present, said by the National Trust to be one of the best private museums in the country. It is certainly well worth a visit. The final building of interest on this walk is a few yards along the road, and it is a large sixteenth century house, refaced during the eighteenth century, and with five large vases up on the roof. There are dummy windows too, and it was originally the town house of the Bromley family who were Lords of the Manor for nearly 300 years.

The Pepperpot

18

Downstream to the Hams

This will be a comfortable two hour walk on mainly flat ground, though it can be muddy in winter, and of course the riverside meadows will be flooded for a few days each year.

Distance: 4 or 5 miles (6.5 or 8 km).
Maps: Landranger 150; Explorer 190.
Car Parking: See walk 17, page 91.
Public Transport: See walk 17, page 91.
Start/Finish: Car park at GR850407.
Refreshments: See walk 17, page 91.

EAVE the Upton upon Severn car park and turn right along the road. Pass the eighteenth century Church Cottages, the Pepperpot and the Heritage Centre, before turning left at the corner, towards the Riverside. On the corner is the old market cross which became the War Memorial and has an interesting eighteenth century sundial near the top. A few yards along the wall towards the River Severn are two diamond shaped plaques commemorating the massive floods of November 14th 1852 and May 15th 1886.

At the river bank, below the car park of the King's Head, notice the circular area which was formerly the location of the turning mechanism of a swing bridge.

Turn right along the river bank, passing the old warehouses and then the Swan Hotel. Lovely trees line the river banks here and for much of the first half of this walk. To the right of the path is Waterside House, a Georgian house converted into flats and beyond this is the Malt House, an even more magnificent Georgian brick built house with a beautiful walled garden, behind the iron gate. Next to it is the King's Stable, a curved Flemish style building which may have been used for keeping horses as long ago as the sixteenth century. Across the river can be seen the large footbridge spanning the entrance to the Marina. The final houses are Severn House and Old Walls, overlooking the site of the old ford across to the east bank. It was near here that the Roundheads crossed the river during the Battle of Upton.

Go through a gate and walk straight on following the river bank, with a huge flood plain, resembling a lake for a few days (or weeks) each winter. This is known as the Hams, a word used to refer to several low lying areas near the Severn and other rivers, and derived from the Old English word for a meadow, especially a flat meadow near a stream. Many wild flowers can be seen along the field margin and river banks during the summer, notably rose bay willow herb, and meadow cranesbill. On the grassy meadow there are large patches of lady's bedstraw.

Turn round occasionally and admire the views of the complete ridge of the Malvern Hills which can be seen to the right, beyond the spire and tower of the two Upton churches. To the left, on the other side of the river can be seen the buildings of the Severn Trent Water Board, one of many places where Severn water is extracted for human use, as well as a former petrol storage depot.

This is a popular river bank for fishermen, and near the line of overhead power cables is a warning notice to remind them of overhead dangers to stray fishing lines and hooks. At the end of the huge field go straight on and at the next stile is the location of the former railway bridge carrying the Malvern-Upton-Tewkesbury line across the Severn. The embankment to keep the line above flood level can be seen extending away to the right, back towards Upton, with a good tree growth on top of it.

The stile has a yellow arrow public footpath and the Severn Way symbol of one of the trows, the trading boats which formerly sailed up and down the Severn. Across the river here is the small hamlet of Saxon's Lode. Continue following the river bank southwards and at the end of the next field go on over the stile, and soon the river has a sharp left bend. The Severn Way continues southwards here, but before reaching a stile and footbridge in the hedge at the end of this field, we turn round to begin the return journey.

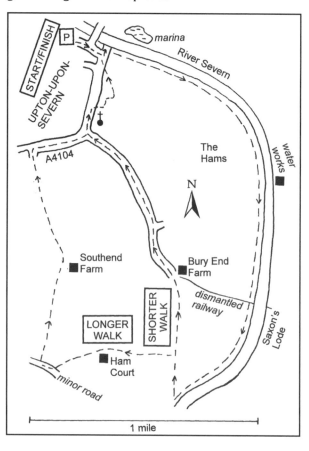

Having turned round, our route is mid way between the river, now on the right, and the hedge, over on the left side of the field about 50 yards away. Head due northwards aiming just to the right of the spire of Upton church. Cross the barbed wire fence at the end of the first field over horizontal wooden poles.

If you want to do the longer five mile walk now continue reading from ★ on page 98. Otherwise ...

... keep straight ahead from the poles. At the end of the field is a stile and beyond this follow the hedge on the right margin of this field. About two-thirds of the way along cross a stile and go forward, now with the hedge on the left. Go through a gate to pass between the farm barns of Buryend Farm. Pass the black and white buildings of the farm on the right and walk straight ahead along the lane.

On reaching the road and the first houses, turn left and walk through the housing estates. The church spire is straight ahead. Pass 'Door Panels plc' on the left and the cemetery on the right, and at the next road turn left, at Hilton, a large eighteenth century house with wrought iron gates and fence. Join the main road by the Fire Station and turn right to walk towards the Parish church. Look across the playing fields to the left and the embankment of the old

The Malt House, Upton

railway line can be seen where it has been cut off at the far side of the fields. The line came straight across the playing fields to the south side of the church, and the railway station was located in what is now the Industrial Estate.

Now continue from ✪ *below.*

★ *For the longer five mile walk, after crossing the wooden poles and the wire fence turn left and go through a gate and out on to a stony drive between hedges. Follow this drive, over a small stream and on to a crossing point of drives, where the magnificent Ham Court is just to the left, surrounded by some fine trees. Keep going straight on to the road, by a few houses.*

Turn right,and after 30 yards turn right again along the driveway to The Close and Close Cottage, following the signpost Public Footpath to Upton. Go through the iron gate and pass the Queenhill W.I., then go through the small kissing gate and into a field. Walk on the left side of the field, alongside the iron fence, with great views of the Malverns over to the left.

At the end of the field bear right to a large gate to exit the field, then go through a small kissing gate, beyond which turn right along the track between the farm buildings of Southend farm. The track bends left and soon joins another very straight track where we turn left. Follow this for half a mile out to the main road, at the Lodge House. Turn right along the road and walk along the pavement to Upton church.

✪ At the parish church of St. Peter and St. Paul, notice the flood level for March 20th 1947 on the gate post at the front of the church. This church was built in 1879 by Arthur Blomfield in a Neo-Gothic style, and its pale yellow stone looks very attractive with the evening sun shining on it. The graceful spire is 183 ft. in height and can be seen from many miles around. Inside the church is the Boteler monument in memory of a Crusader knight member of the Boteler family from Upton. The Corona or Crown hanging overhead is a circle of eight winged figures designed by Anthony Robinson.

After visiting the church, follow Church Walk alongside the church, to the T-junction of paths, and turn left. Before going ahead, look at the fine Rectory building at the back of the church, with its prominent bay windows – at all floors. Walk between the houses for about 40 yards then turn right down another alleyway, and at the road turn left, between the school and the police station. Beyond the school is St. Joseph's Roman Catholic church designed in 1850 by Charles Hansom, who was the brother of the designer of the Hansom cab.

At the end of School Lane on the right side embedded in the side of the road is a piece of basalt, an erratic block thought to have been carried from North Wales by ice during the Ice Age. On the left of this road junction is the Old Court House and round the corner to the left beyond this is Court Row.

Along here on the right side is the chapel in which John Wesley preached in 1770 and nearby is the old Royal Oak Inn, an eighteenth century building.

Retrace your steps along Court Row and continue along Court Street, passing several small shops and an alleyway going through to a courtyard at the rear of these shops. At the main road turn right passing the Talbot Head Hotel and the White Lion Hotel. Before reaching the river, turn left along Church Street to walk back to the starting point of the walk. Just along Church Street look out for the plaque on the wall on the left recording the welcome that Oliver Cromwell received here on 29th August 1651 after the Battle of Upton.

19

Earl's Croome

This walk will require between two and three hours. The outward journey is across farm land, and the return is along the river bank.

Distance: Just over 5 miles (8 km).
Maps: Landranger 150; Explorer 190.
Car Parking: See walk 17, page 91
Public Transport: Bus service 363/364 between Worcester and Great Malvern calls at Upton upon Severn.
Start/Finish: Car park near the bridge at GR850407.
Refreshments: See walk 17, page 91.

L EAVE the Upton upon Severn car park, turn right along the road and then go left over the bridge. The earliest reference to a bridge was in a 1480 document which mentions a wooden bridge. Previously, crossing the River Severn here was by ferry, or by the ford a short distance downstream. The first stone bridge was built in 1605-09. Floods destroyed the bridge in 1872, and an iron swing bridge was then built. The present structure was built in 1940.

Once across the river, walk along the pavement for a quarter mile, and to the left are the flat fields of the flood plain and to the right is the Marina. The road has flood marker posts, an indication of what might happen in the winter. Road works during 2005 raised the road level to reduce the flood risk.

Where the main road bends to the right, turn left by Ryall Chase and The Rag House, along a bridleway to get away from the noise of traffic. This is initially a surfaced drive, but beyond a gate it becomes a stony track along the right margin of a field. The track turns into Holly Green Severn Trent station, but we walk straight on, through another gate and passing to the right of a small pond.

Turn right at the end of this field, just before reaching the buildings of Ryalls Court Farm, so that the duck pond is to the left. Cross over a surfaced driveway and then pass the side of a small pond to follow the hedge on the left margin of the field. At the end of the field go through an old iron kissing gate and keep straight ahead along the left of the next field. Go over a stile, to a cross paths, but keep straight on, over the next stile. Head diagonally across the next field by passing just to the right of the tree in the middle. Once over the stile at the end of this field follow the gravel driveway down to the stile on

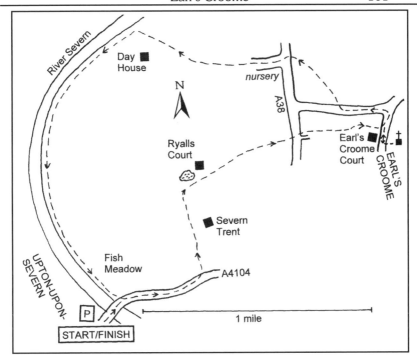

the right side of a shed and a barn, then go over another stile by a gate to reach the road, the A38.

Directly across the road is the entrance to the seventeenth century Earl's Croome Court, with its tree lined avenue. Our path is just to the left of this, near the right margin of the field, but gradually moving left further into the field, unless there is a crop which might necessitate following round the right side of the field. On the fence at the far end is a stile and continue across the next small field to a stile in the left corner, near a pond. Go over the stile and turn right to follow the hedge and walk out to the road. The fine building of the Court is over the wall to the right.

At the road go over the stile and turn right to visit the twelfth century church of St. Nicholas, with its squat tower. In the churchyard is a large tomb for Charles John Coventry, second son of the Ninth Earl of Coventry. From the church retrace steps along the road, to pass the old school with a date of 1856, the village hall on the right, and then old cottages built by the Ninth Earl of Coventry in1879.

Turn left at the road junction and walk on out of the village. On the right is a footpath leading alongside the last house, and through to a stile. Go over the stile and head diagonally left across a large field, to pass the willow trees at the corner of the next field. There is a small pond near this corner. Keep straight ahead in a north westerly direction, along the same line and pass through a gap in the hedge, at the far side of the next field, and over a small ditch. Continue still in the same direction past the corner of a garden and on to the stile by the gate, and the main road A38 again.

Turn left along the road for about 30 yards and then right along a driveway, just before reaching the Earl's Croome Nursery and Garden Centre. Follow the track between hedges, often in a vegetation tunnel with trees growing and meeting overhead. In places there are remnants of brick paving on this track, placed there to prevent the pack donkeys from walking in too much mud. This track formerly led down to a landing stage on the river. It narrows to a path and begins to go downhill slightly, and eventually reaches an old iron gate.

Go through the gate, and continue straight along the track. Views of Day House, formerly two small cottages, may be seen to the left, and straight ahead on the other side of the river can be seen the superb building of Severn End, the home of the Lechmere family for more than 700 years. The old house was badly damaged by fire in 1896, but has been rebuilt in a similar style. The Malvern Ridge makes a magnificent backcloth to the view.

Pass through a small gate and turn right for a few yards to get down to the river, and then turn left along the river bank to walk back to Upton. The river is on the right, and to your left is a small embankment which may stop small floods from spreading over the river meadows, but will not prevent large floods. These often spread half mile or so across towards Ryalls Court which is located just out of reach of most flood waters. The church spire and Pepperpot can be seen ahead and to the left, showing that we have a large bend of the river to follow back to our starting point.

Over to the right is Severn End House and on the river bank is its boathouse.

At the end of the first field, turn round and look back upstream, and just above the trees can be seen the fine building of Severn Bank, a large early nineteenth century house, near the village of Severn Stoke.

Go over a stile and straight on, passing the marker post with a footpath sign on it and also the trow symbol for the Severn Way. There are brush wood jumps in this field, for the Point to Point which takes place here on Easter Tuesday and in August . The river and the boats can be seen, as well as birds such as gulls, swallows, ducks, swans at different times of the year, and an occasional sighting of a kingfisher. Curlews may be heard in these riverside meadows.

To the right, across on the other bank is the end of Quay Lane at Hanley Castle, and the old warehouse which is now a house, all that is left of the buildings handling former river traffic. To the left views are restricted by the flood embankment, unless you move a few yards left and walk on top of this small ridge. From here are excellent views across the meadows to Ryalls Court and Earl's Croome and the farmland on the sloping margin of the Severn valley.

Just keep following the river through the flood meadows, to the final field which is called Fish Meadow. Bear left to go through the underpass below the main road, and up on to the bridge. Cross the bridge to return to the starting point.

Upton, the church and the Pepperpot

20

A Ramble to Ripple

Some picturesque villages, with fine views of the Malverns and Bredon Hill on a fairly level walk.

Distance: 7 miles (11 km).
Maps: Landranger 150; Explorer 190.
Car Parking: See walk 17, page 91.
Public Transport: See walk 17, page 91.
Start/Finish: Car park near the bridge at GR850407.
Refreshments: See walk 17, page 91 Also a pub in Ripple.

TURN RIGHT from the Upton upon Severn car park and then left across the river bridge. Once across the river, turn right along the tarmac path and walk past the picnic site. Just past this an abutment of a former bridge can be seen, opposite the Kings Head. Go right along a driveway between the two houses, Bridge End House and Bridge End Cottage. This leads to the high footbridge over the entrance to Upton Marina. Keep straight ahead, with the marina to the left and the river to the right. Note the flood level gauge in the river.

The River Severn has always been important to Upton, now because of the pleasure traffic but formerly as a trading route. As early as the thirteenth century Upton had already become a port, and handled trade not only to towns further up the Severn, but also for the Bishop of Hereford. River traffic increased steadily and the Severn was one of Europe's busiest river routes in the seventeenth and eighteenth centuries.

Go through a gate and along the river embankment through a large grassy field, and at the end of this meadow, pass through a metal kissing-gate and climb gently up a narrow path, bearing right when the path divides at the top of the rise. Turn left at the road to pass a few new bungalows and then older houses before reaching the road B4212.

Turn right along this road for 50 yards and where the road bends left, take the driveway which is alongside Ryall House Farm. There are large mushroom shaped, red sandstone, staddle stones at the right of this drive, and the footpath sign is hidden by a tree. Staddle stones were once used to support barns and granaries, keeping them off the ground and allowing air to circulate. The overlap would have kept out rats and mice.

Follow this drive passing the recently modernised buildings and over a stile by a double wooden gate. Walk on, with the hedge and fence to the right, and

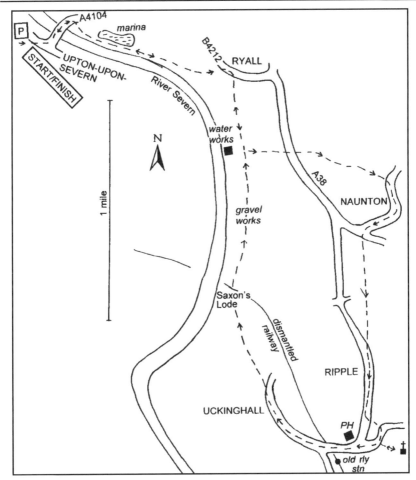

then over another stile by a metal gate. Keep straight on with the hedge now on the left, and approach the area of gravel extraction, a surprising piece of industrial development in such a rural landscape. The gravel is probably a relic of deposition associated with flooding by an enlarged River Severn carrying meltwater and rock debris during the Ice Age. Extraction will continue for a few years, but the landscape will be restored when the work is completed. Meanwhile a public footpath is maintained through the gravel pits, though this does not now correspond to that shown in the OS map.

Once level with the Severn Trent building (fronted by a green tank) on the right, turn left, over a stile and across the gravel workings, going parallel to the drive leading to the Water Company's building. At the main road A38, cross over to take a good staircase stile on to the path following alongside a hedge to the right, and then go diagonally to the far right corner of the next field.

Go over another stile and turn left alongside the hedge, and at the end of this field, head diagonally right across the next field to the far corner, aiming just to the right of a wooden fence. This will lead out on to a narrow road, in the small hamlet of Naunton.

Turn right past the telephone box and walk along the road. Where it splits turn right and keep going as far as the main road, the A38 again. Cross over and bend slightly left, go over the stile and follow the hedge on your right.

Pass to the right of the modern buildings of a Veterinary Surgeon, go through a paddock, cross a narrow road and go straight on across the next field. Here as in many places on this walk, there are wonderful views of the Malvern Hills in one direction, and Bredon Hill in the opposite.

Reach a narrow road near the buildings of Ripple Farm, and continue straight along the road, passing the parish hall and arriving in the village of Ripple. Where the road bends right by a house with an old fashioned lamp post in the garden, go left over a stile and along a short narrow path.

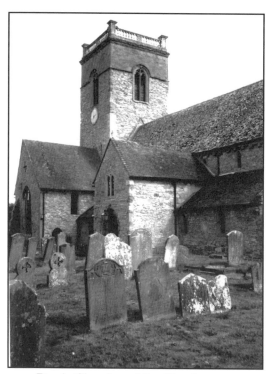

Ripple Church and the Giant's grave

Turn right along the edge of the field, at the back of the houses, and at the end of this field turn right along the road. Where the road turns right, which is our way ahead, turn left passing the Rectory, in order to visit the church.

The remarkable church of St. Mary, dates from 1190, and is transitional in style, between Norman and Early English. It is on the site of an early Saxon church from AD680, and formerly had a ninth century monastery next door. The church is built of light coloured stone, with some red sandstone and is most famous for its fine set of sixteen fifteenth century misericords, of which twelve depict the year in the

Misericord in Ripple Church

countryside. In the porch is a lepers' trough, and in the churchyard is the grave of the Ripple Giant, Robert Reeve, who died of a heart attack in 1626 after mowing Uckinghall Meadow in a day, for a wager.

Ripple is a very old settlement, dating back to Roman times. It was formerly much more important than Upton, and was a manor of the Bishop of Worcester. In the Civil War a major battle was fought here in 1643.

From the church walk back to the road and pass the old fourteenth century preaching cross and the village stocks, surrounded by a group of tiny cottages. This was the meeting place of ancient routes from Bredon, Malvern, Worcester and Tewkesbury.

A few yards along the road is The Old Forge, with a clock on its wall, and just beyond this is a huge old barn. Walk on past the Railway Inn, and leave the village, going over the old railway bridge. The former branch line from Upton to Tewkesbury went through here, and a few yards to the left is the station building which is now a private house.

The road splits at the bridge and we fork right to walk through the picturesque village of Uckinghall, with some delightful houses and gardens backed with a fine view of the Malverns. Pass a tiny green with the remnants of an old cross on it, and ignore the left turn to the river, keeping straight ahead. Look out for the thatch peacocks on the roof of a thatched cottage and then, at a second thatched cottage where the road bends right, go straight ahead along the stony drive (signposted Footpath to Ryall), and pass over a stile and to the left of the farm buildings.

Follow the right margin of this field with a hedge on the right, then over another stile and alongside the hedge again. When the hedge ends go straight

The Railway Inn, Ripple

ahead across the middle of the field to another stile. Cross the drive leading left, to the farm complex of Saxon's Lode, named after Sexton and not the early Saxons. There are Sextons buried in Ripple churchyard.

Go straight ahead across the next field, over a stile and across the line of the old railway, and then over another stile to the left of an iron fence. There is the evidence of an old oil storage depot here, a relic of the time when river tankers brought oil up the Severn.

Turn left alongside the line of the old railway, then right along a stony track. Follow this through the gravel workings. The exact location of these workings may change in the next few years, but we can expect the footpath to be clearly shown.

The path leads back to the Severn Trent buildings passed on the outward journey and you now just retrace your steps back into Upton upon Severn. Go forward with the hedge first on the right, then on the left to reach the road. Go along this for about 50 yards and then left along Ryall Meadow. Where this road swings sharply left go through the kissing gate and follow the path to the right to reach the river. Then walk along the riverside and over the Marina bridge back to your starting point.

Index

More walks from Meridian...

A YEAR OF WALKS IN THE THREE CHOIRS COUNTIES by Roy Woodcock

The Three Choirs Counties comprise Herefordshire, Gloucestershire and Worcestertshire and this selection of walks takes twelve widely distributed locations, one for each month of the year.

£6.95. ISBN 1-869922-51-4. 112 pages. 28 illustrations. 12 maps

WALKS IN SEVERN COUNTRY by Roy Woodcock

The River Severn, Britain's longest river, rises on Plynlimon in Wales and flows through the beautiful counties of Powys, Shropshire, Worcestershire and Gloucestershire before discharging into the Bristol Channel. In this book the author presents twenty walks that explore some of the fine towns and countryside that the Severn passes through on its 220 mile journey to the sea.

£7.95. ISBN 1-869922-49-2. 128 pages. 37 illustrations. 20 maps

HERITAGE DISCOVERY WALKS IN THE MIDLANDS by Peter Groves

Britain has a rich historical heritage and the twenty-one walks in this book explore some fine Midlands countryside and also present opportunities to visit castles, battlefields, nature reserves, museums, churches and cathedrals; to admire fine architecture and to explore some historic towns. And there are some excellent pubs, many with interesting histories.

They are all circular and accessible by public transport. The shortest is 2½ miles/ 4km; the longest 11¼ miles/18 km.

£6.95. ISBN 1-869922-50-6. 160 pages. 52 illustrations. 20 maps

WALKS TO WET YOUR WHISTLE by Roger Seedhouse

Eighteen walks covering some of the most beautiful countryside in Shropshire and along its Staffordshire borders, each providing an opportunity to visit a pub in which the walker will feel welcome and comfortable.

£6.95. ISBN 1 869922 41 7. 112 pages. 17 photographs. 18 maps.

MORE WALKS TO WET YOUR WHISTLE by Roger Seedhouse

A second collection of walks with a pub in Shropshire and along its Staffordshire borders.

£6.95. ISBN 1 869922 36 0. 112 pages. 24 photographs. 18 maps.

WARWICKSHIRE WALKS TO WET YOUR WHISTLE by Roger Seedhouse

Roger Seedhouse's third collection of walks, all with good pubs, in Warwickshire – a land of lakes and country parks which are a delight to behold, merging into the Northern Cotswolds with its buildings of honey-hued stone.

£8.95. ISBN 1-869922-48-4 120 pages 21 photos 20 maps

WALKS THROUGH HISTORY IN THE HEART OF ENGLAND by Roger Seedhouse

The Heart of England is rich in history, both ancient and more modern, and the twenty-four walks in this book will offer the enquiring walker many intriguing glimpses of a bygone age – with iron-age forts, battle sites, medieval castles and even a second world war camp. All of them start at, or pass through, places of historical interest that will add greatly to your appreciation of a day out in beautiful walking country.

£8.95 ISBN 1-869922-41-7. 160 pages. 38 photos. 24 maps.

WALKING WITH THE FAMOUS ... AND THE INFAMOUS by Roger Seedhouse

A unique book of fifteen walks in Shropshire through areas associated with some of the county's most colourful historical characters. In an original and distinctive style the walks also relate the principal events of the character's lives and are written as if through their own eyes.

£8.95. ISBN 1-869922-46-8. 128 pages. 15 maps. Illustrated with photos and drawings.

WALKS IN SOUTH WARWICKSHIRE: FROM SHAKESPEARE COUNTRY TO THE COTSWOLDS by John W Parnham and Barry R Wills

This collection of circular walks represent the authors' favourites within this lovely, varied region. The walks will take you along ancient trackways and paths, past standing stones, earthworks, country estates and grand houses. In the Arden countryside as well as finding connections to William Shakespeare you will discover hidden valleys and distinct wooded hilltops that offer wonderful views. Further south the walks will take you through delightful villages and into remote areas in the Cotswold Hills that rival in many ways the better known parts of this beautiful region.

£6.95. ISBN 1 869922 38 7. 112 pages. 36 sketches. 18 maps.

A TEME VALLEY WALK by David Milton

The Teme is one of the most beautiful and fast-flowing rivers in the country but remains quite secretive for much of its length. This long distance walk remains as dose as possible to the river but takes to the hills where footpaths, public transport or accommodation needs dictate. It starts in Worcester and ends, after visiting the source of the river, in Newtown, a total distance of 93 miles.

£8.95. ISBN 1-869922-45-X. 176 pages. 22 illustrations. 17 maps.

THE RIVERSIDES WAY by David Milton

A 70 mile circular walk in the area of the Welsh Marches immediately to the south and west of Ludlow. Centred on Aymestry it takes in the valleys and surrounding hills of the two rivers that drain the region – the Teme, in the north, and the Lugg, in the south.

£8.95. ISBN 1-869922-43-3. 160 pages. 13 photos. 14 maps.

THE ELAN VALLEY WAY by David Milton

The Elan Valley Way runs from Frankley, on the western fringe of Birmingham, to the Elan Valley in mid-Wales. It is loosely based around the course followed by the Elan Valley aqueduct along which Birmingham's water supply has passed since 1904. Largely following footpaths and bridleways, and with many superb views, the 128½ mile route passes through some delightful walking areas in the counties of Worcestershire, Shropshire, Herefordshire and Powys.

£7.95. ISBN 1 869922 39 5. 160 pages. 21 photographs. 21 maps.

THE BIRMINGHAM GREENWAY by Fred Willits

A walk from the northern to the southern boundary of Birmingham passing through its many parks and open spaces, using footpaths, riversides and canal towpaths. A unique opportunity to discover what is often hidden to the road user and to learn much about the history and current activities of this bustling city.

£4.95. ISBN 1 869922 40 9. 64 pages. 33 photographs. 3 drawings. 10 strip maps.

All Meridian titles are available from booksellers or, if in difficulty, direct from the publishers.

Please send your remittance, including the following amounts for postage and packing:
Order value up to £10.00 add £1.50;
over £10.00 and up to £20.00 add £2.50;
over £20.00 add £3.00.

Meridian Books
Sales Office
8 Hartside Close, Lutley, Halesowen, West Midlands B63 1HP
Tel: 0121-429 4397
e-mail: meridian.books@tiscali.co.uk

Please send for our complete catalogue of walking guides covering both local and long distance walks.